1795

# STARR

# My Life in Football

# STARR

# BART STARR

## with Murray Olderman

WILLIAM MORROW AND COMPANY, INC.
NEW YORK

Library of Congress Cataloging-in-Publication Data

Starr, Bart.
Starr: the story of my life in football/by Bart Starr, with
Murray Olderman.
p.    cm.
ISBN 0-688-06752-2
1. Starr, Bart. 2. Football players—United States—Biography.
I. Olderman, Murray. II. Title.
GV939.S73A3 1987
796.332'092'4—dc19
[b]                          87-19847
                                   CIP

Printed in the United States of America

First Edition

1 2 3 4 5 6 7 8 9 10

BOOK DESIGN BY PATRICE FODERO

This book is dedicated to
the loving memory of my brother and my father.
And to my mother, wife, and children,
whose devotion has always
given me strength in the face of adversity.
Each has given
special meaning to my life.

With great appreciation to those teammates whose support throughout my career contributed to the success I enjoyed. To Murray Olderman, who worked so closely with me and compiled much of the material used in this book. A special thanks to Bart junior and his associate, John Gustafson, and their secretaries, Pam and Debbie, for the long hours of editing and researching, which helped make this book possible.

# INTRODUCTION

A microcosm of my football life occurred in Green Bay, Wisconsin, on December 31, 1967. During three hours on an arctic sheet of frozen turf, I encountered adversity, elation, despair, and exhilaration. Humiliation would arrive sixteen years later.

While the rest of the country was warming up to celebrate the New Year, the Green Bay Packers were preparing to host the Dallas Cowboys in what would be one of the coldest games in the history of professional football. The temperature at kickoff read 13 below; strong winds caused the chill factor to register minus 46. The press-box windows, clouded by condensation from breathing and coffee, were soon covered with ice. Tom Miller, the Packers' business manager, saw little of the game, since he spent the afternoon scraping off the ice. The Dallas Cowboys' big threat at wide receiver was Bob Hayes, the Olympic sprinting champion. On this day, however, he couldn't run because his hands were tucked in his pants. Tony Franklin and Rich Karlis would have begged for shoes in those conditions.

Coach Vince Lombardi prohibited us from wearing an excessive amount of underclothing, because he believed it restricted our movement. But even he wore long underwear on that day. Every player would have welcomed the skintight gloves so prevalent now. Had they been available, I might have avoided frostbite. I still shiver when I hear the words "Ice Bowl."

Imagine how difficult it was to ignore the elements and concentrate on the most important play in Packer history. With sixteen seconds remaining in the 1967 NFL championship game, I called our final timeout. We had possession of the ball 2 feet from the Dallas goal line. The Cowboys led, 17–14, but we were in the driver's seat.

My concern about the icy turf prompted me to ask Jerry Kramer, our all-pro right guard, "Can you get your footing for a wedge play?"

"Hell, yes!" he confidently shot back through the roar of the crowd.

I turned and jogged to the sideline to plot strategy with Coach Lombardi. A field goal would have tied the game and forced a sudden-death overtime. But it never crossed his mind . . . the time to win was now.

On the two previous downs, which began inside the Cowboys' 2-yard line, we ran a short-yardage, straight-ahead play known as a wedge. On first down, Donny Anderson gained a yard; on second down, a foot. Although our blocking was sound, our running backs could not accelerate without slipping. However, I had better footing near the line of scrimmage, where the ice had been broken from the activity in the trenches.

"I can sneak the ball in," I said to Lombardi.

"Then run it in," he growled. "Let's get the hell out of here."

We now had only one opportunity to win, because our decision to run the ball meant that the game would end if we failed. The key to our success would be our ability to drive Jethro Pugh off the line of scrimmage. Pugh, the Cowboys' left tackle, was a solid player, but he occasionally came off the ball too high during short yardage situations. The burden rested with Ken Bowman, our center, and Jerry to form a wedge and knock Pugh into the end zone. Forrest Gregg, our outstanding right tackle, had to prevent Larry Cole, their left end, from jamming the middle. As we broke from the huddle, I knew we would score. The crowd noise was deafening and I instinctively raised both arms to request silence. But time seemed to stand still. . . . I heard nothing at all. I saw the frosty breath from aching lungs on both sides of the line. With a deliberate short count, I initiated the most significant play of my life. Our linemen executed their assignments to perfection, and I tunneled into the end zone behind Ken and Jerry's effective blocks. Jerry and I received more publicity from that play than we had our entire careers. Ken's contribution, which was also critical, was somehow overlooked. What left a more lasting impression in my mind, however, was the sequence of events leading up to the touchdown.

We would not have faced that goal-line dilemma had we protected our 14–0 lead. Wide receiver Boyd Dowler and I connected for two touchdown passes, but the Cowboys rallied, capitalizing on two nearly disastrous turnovers. The first occurred when I was stripped of the ball while scrambling. Defensive end George Andrie scooped it up and lumbered 20 yards into the end zone. The second turnover resulted from Willie Wood's muff of a fair-catch attempt. Dallas converted this opportunity into a field goal. On the first play of the fourth quarter, the Cowboys took the lead, 17–14, as a result of a remarkable play. Halfback Dan Reeves swept left, skidded to a near stop, pivoted, and threw a sidearm, tight spiral that landed in the arms of Lance Rentzel at the Packer 10-yard line. Reeves's execution of the option pass was so skillful he completely deceived every defensive player on our team. By the time strong safety Tom Brown realized Reeves was going to pass, Rentzel was already 15 yards behind him.

With five minutes remaining in the game, we gained possession on our 32-yard line. With conditions steadily worsening, we knew this would probably be our last opportunity to mount a sustained drive. Everyone in our huddle was composed and confident. I looked in their eyes, called the play, and said, "This is it. Let's get it done."

It took us only three completions to reach the Dallas 30-yard line. Following a clutch reception by Dowler, Donny Anderson, our halfback, noticed that the Cowboys were not covering him as he came out of our backfield. He said, "Bart, if you'll dump the ball off to me, I can pick up eight or ten yards every play." I took his advice and let Donny skate through the Cowboy defense for two consecutive plays.

Chuck Mercein, our fullback from Yale, was also a perceptive ballplayer. He observed that the Cowboys were double-covering wide receiver Carroll Dale, and told me he could sneak into the opening behind Carroll. As I dropped back to pass, I saw the Dallas defenders converge on Carroll, just as Chuck said they would. He hauled in the pass and scrambled 19 yards before stumbling out of bounds at the 11.

In my opinion, the next play was the best I ever called under pressure. I knew that Bob Lilly, the Cowboys' all-pro tackle, would pursue laterally when the opposing guard pulled. His amazing quickness and intelligence allowed him to run down ball carriers on sweeps, but it also occasionally left Dallas vulnerable if their other linemen failed to "cover" for him. George Andrie, their right end, was responsible for filling the gap left by Lilly's pursuit. Before the play I asked our left tackler, Bob Skoronski, if he could prevent Andrie from coming inside. He had no doubt he could. In the huddle, I called, "Thirty give," which was an influence play designed to deceive the defense into thinking we were running a sweep. Our left guard, Gale Gillingham, pulled to the right; Lilly followed and took himself out of the play. Bob Skoronski made his block on Andrie as I handed the ball to Mercein, who plunged straight ahead through the gaping hole for 8 yards. Three plays later, we wrapped up our third-straight NFL title.

Earlier in my career, many fans misinterpreted my calm demeanor for lack of imagination. They believed that Lombardi programmed me to follow his orders and not worry about originality. But by the time we executed our winning championship drive, I had become a creative and confident leader who could stand beside, not behind, our admired coach.

# CHAPTER

## 1

*"The law that I have preached—and the discipline that have established, will be your master after my disappearance."*

—DIGHA NIKAYA, II

Vince Lombardi was a tough and mercurial drillmaster. People have often asked me whether it was difficult to tolerate his tirades, mood swings, and criticism. When I tell them it was not, they raise their eyebrows as if to say, "You must be kidding."

I had been conditioned to handle a tougher personality much earlier in my life.

I was raised in a military family under the hand, figuratively and literally, of a domineering master sergeant, Ben Starr. Although my dad's family lived in Anniston, in northern Alabama, he was born in Dadeville, a small town in the red-clay country of central Alabama. His great-grandfather was a full-blooded Cherokee Indian, and Dad's striking features—a square jaw, high cheekbones, and dark hair—were characteristic of his unique ancestry. In addition, his later employment as a blacksmith, a mechanic, and a welder helped him develop a muscular torso. My father's parents died when he was seven; his grandfather adopted him and instilled in him a pride in his Indian heritage. He was a down-to-earth Southerner who was forced to quit high school during the Depression. However, he later received his diploma while in the service, and it meant as much to him as my college degree did to me.

My mother, the former Lulu Inez Tucker, was born in Deatsville, Alabama, a rural area eighteen miles from Montgomery. When she was three, her family moved to the city. Her father was a railroad engineer and later a reformatory guard. My parents met while my mother was visiting a friend whom my father had once dated in Anniston. They quickly fell in love and were married three and a half months later, in October 1932.

Dad's background helped him land a job as a blacksmith with American Ice and Coal Company in Montgomery. I was born on January 9, 1934, and named Bryan Bartlett Starr. "Bryan" was my father's middle name; Haywood Bartlett was the obstetrician who delivered me (in more recent years, I have been amused by letters from devoted fans indicating they had named their son, Bartholemew, after me). My brother, Hilton, whom we called "Bubba," was born two years later.

When I was three, we moved to Columbia, Tennessee, where my father worked for Monsanto Chemical Company, but we returned to Montgomery shortly before I entered first grade. Dad had accepted a position with the Alabama highway department, supervising prisoner work details. Shortly after the United States entered World War II, his National Guard unit was mobilized.

For two years, we lived in Gainesville, Florida, while Dad was based at Fort Blanding. We then moved to Fort Ord, on the Monterey peninsula of California. Nearby Carmel's natural beauty left a lasting impression on me. Hilton and I spent hours watching the powerful surf crash against the base of the cliffs that lined the rugged coastline. Carmel was unspoiled then; the residents had yet to experience spaghetti westerns or Dirty Harry.

We lived in Ord Village, a clustered military community

between Salinas and Monterey. I remember waiting with Hilton in the evening for Dad to return home in his jeep. When he stopped at the gate, we jumped in and rode the short distance to our "barracks." This was the consummate thrill. Even Dad looked forward to our daily ritual.

In 1942 he entered the Pacific combat zone, and we didn't see him again for four years. I never fully understood the significance of my father's absence until Hilton and I visited the Empire theater one afternoon. A Fox Movietone newsreel documenting MacArthur's dramatic return to the Philippines preceded the main attraction. "Hey, Bubba, that looks like Dad behind MacArthur," I said.

"Nah," he scoffed.

"Sure it is. Look!"

We sat through Gene Autry's *Cowboy Serenade* three times before Bubba was convinced. When our father returned home, he verified the fact that he had been among the troops at Mindanao.

The war accentuated his stern demeanor. He was hardened and demanding. He became a career military man and transferred to the air force as a noncommissioned career officer. He ran our household as he did his squadron—he was my master sergeant. I was not allowed to express my own views or disagree with him. I never even raised my voice. He intimidated me.

Dad decided we would live in Montgomery permanently. Although he knew he might have to serve some tours of duty, he wanted us to grow up in a stable environment so our schooling wouldn't be interrupted.

We lived in a white-frame house, which Dad had purchased for $3,500. It was located on a deep, narrow lot on National Avenue in a middle-income neighborhood. It may have been small, but in our eyes it was a dream house. Dad's Chevy barely fit into the detached garage. I can't count the number of pennies I lost betting Hilton that Dad was going to scrape his car pulling in or backing out.

Very few Southern homes had air conditioning in the 1940s, and I couldn't imagine anything more intolerable than

Alabama's heat and humidity (until I experienced my first winter in northern Wisconsin). During the sticky summer nights, the still, wet air became an oppressive blanket. It usually took at least an hour for me to fall asleep, dreading the sweat-soaked sheets I'd find in the morning. When my parents finally bought some small floor fans, and later window fans, the air was still warm but at least moving. Dad eventually bought an attic fan and I was convinced we were in heaven.

Despite the summertime weather, I enjoyed growing up in Montgomery. Hilton and I were fortunate to live in a neighborhood with other kids our age, and, though we lacked formal leagues through which we could compete in sports, we had no shortage of imagination.

Baseball was our favorite game; finding a ballpark was our challenge. We used sickles to cut the high grass and weeds, then mowed an area large enough to stake out base paths. In the summer, we gathered after breakfast and played until sunset. We were infuriated when construction began on a vacant lot we had converted into a diamond. Eventually we found another field and headed for our garages to grab the sickles.

In the fall, base paths became sidelines. We played tackle football without pads or headgear. Although we suffered occasional scrapes and bruises, no one was seriously hurt. But that was during the week. On Saturday, we held our "championship game" in front of an imaginary crowd at Hurt Military Academy. The competition was intense. We returned home with bleeding elbows and a greater love for the game.

Success on the playing field was tremendously important in our family. For Dad, it was everything. In his youth, he had had little time for team sports because he had to work to support himself and his grandfather. He recaptured his youth vicariously through our participation. However, he felt that my brother, not I, was destined for athletic greatness. Bubba's personality mirrored Dad's. A natural athlete with a blazing desire and volatile temper, Bubba was aggressive, with a mean streak. I was an introvert. I suppressed my feelings. I noticed the attention Bubba received from Dad, resented it, and became determined to prove to my father that I, too, could excel.

My mother, however, never favored either of us. She was always loving and caring. She was also a great cook. Her Southern vegetables, country-fried steak, and coconut pie still bring back warm memories from my childhood. The importance of strong family ties was something she emphasized to us. On many weekends, we drove to Anniston to visit my father's relatives. We attended church in the morning, played softball in the afternoon, and then feasted on a large meal. These trips brought our family closer together. When I was thirteen, however, a tragedy nearly ripped us apart.

Despite our conflicting personalities, I loved and admired my brother. We were inseparable. After returning from church one Sunday, we were playing tag with the kids next door. The weather was warm, our feet bare. Racing around the corner of our house, Hilton suddenly screamed. An old dog bone protruding from the grass had pierced his heel. His foot became severely infected. He contracted tetanus and died three days later.

I was devastated. For years, I felt guilty about resenting the attention that Bubba had received from Dad.

A week after my brother died, my father had to leave for a tour of duty in Japan. I will never forget the lonely look of despair on his face and bitterness in his voice when he said good-bye. Mom and I had to bear the loss without his support. I remember the long, lonely hours spent in my room brooding over Bubba's death. My mother felt overwhelming guilt because of the circumstances following the accident. She dearly loved Bubba and was reluctant to bring him in for a tetanus shot, which was a relatively new medical development, but which, it ended up, would have saved his life. It took years for us to overcome the tragedy. Our family still avoids discussing it, but a vivid memory remains.

When my father returned from Japan, I thought our relationship would improve. It deteriorated. Bubba was no longer around for Dad to point to as an example of what I should strive for. He didn't believe I could excel unless I adopted my brother's personality, and constantly prodded me with pointed comments that began, "Your brother would have . . ."

I didn't understand his intentions. But I also detected his new, heightened interest in my development. He understood my affinity for sports, and spent many hours after work playing baseball with me to help improve my fundamental skills. The most memorable gift I received was the baseball glove he bought on my fourteenth birthday. Montgomery had a minor league team in the South Atlantic League; he took me to nearly every game. Dad had a second job at the ballpark as ticket taker. I was a ball boy. During pitching duels I would imagine that Bob Feller was on the mound facing Ted Williams and Joe DiMaggio.

The "Yankee Clipper" was my childhood hero. I traveled to Detroit by bus to visit my Aunt Myrtle and see the Yankees play the Tigers. I saved as much money as possible, but the cost of the bus ticket meant I sat in bleacher seats so cheap that only Bob Uecker could appreciate them. As I watched DiMaggio perform his magic, I thought how unfair it was that he missed three seasons during the prime of his career because of military obligations. The Tiger fans reminded me that Hank Greenberg had to serve his country, too. But I wanted to see Joe hit safely in fifty-seven straight games, and I was sure he would have broken his old record right in front of me. His best years were now behind him, but he never disappointed. Not even a hitless afternoon could quell my enthusiasm; I knew Joe would start a new streak the next day.

In the summer of 1946, while, along with thousands of others, I watched Joe's historic feats, I never considered the fact that every fan in the stadium had been robbed of the opportunity to cheer for players potentially as great as Greenberg or DiMaggio. Branch Rickey had yet to make his courageous move. The names Robinson, Irvin, Doby, Campanella, and Newcombe were unfamiliar to me.

Montgomery was completely segregated in the 1940s. My father never specifically prohibited me from associating with blacks, but the city's unwritten rules made that warning unnecessary. I finally discovered how deeply rooted his prejudice was during the next summer in Detroit, when we drove there in his Chevy.

After watching the Yankees battle the Tigers, I played in pickup games in nearby sandlots. One afternoon, Dad decided to see how much my skills had improved. When he discovered that our contests were integrated, he yanked me off the field, brought me to Aunt Myrtle's house, and punished me by making me wash and rewash his car in the midday sun. His military career had broadened his viewpoint, but it would be years before he became more openminded. Ironically, his greatest progress occurred during his visits to Green Bay—a city with no permanent black residents at that time—when he met such teammates as Willie Davis, Herb Adderley, Elijah Pitts, and Willie Wood.

Each fall, Dad and I shifted our focus from baseball to football. I enjoyed playing pickup games, but was not a diehard fan, mainly because I had yet to see anyone dominate and control a football game. I became hooked, however, one afternoon at the Crampton Bowl in Montgomery. The University of Alabama was playing, and they featured a spectacular tailback named Harry Gilmer. His ability to execute the jump pass led him to the NFL, where he played and coached for many years. I had found a new hero, a new goal. I wanted to throw the football as well as Harry.

Our first organized team, in the eighth grade, was sponsored by VFW Post No. 96. The following year, at Baldwin Junior High, I started as a wingback, in the Notre Dame "box" formation developed by Knute Rockne, their legendary coach. As a runner, blocker, and receiver, I was involved in plenty of action, but obviously I was in the wrong position.

I entered Sidney Lanier High School in tenth grade and became a T-formation quarterback. I was thrilled. Our coach, Bill Moseley, was an upbeat, knowledgeable disciple of Kentucky's Bear Bryant. He was a perfect choice for head coach.

I almost missed my chance of a lifetime, however, before my dad straightened me out.

During the first few weeks of practice, I decided to give up football. I knew I was better than the backup quarterbacks but was already relegated to the junior varsity. Frustrated over the coach's decision, I strolled into our house and told my father I was quitting. I had a list of reasons for my decision and was prepared for his emotional response. Instead, he calmly replied, "All right, it's your decision. I'm glad you'll be home in the afternoons. I want you to weed the garden and cut the cornstalks. I want the garden cleaned up for fall." Dad knew how much I hated that garden—it was 150 feet long and 50 feet wide. At practice the next day, I was the first player on the field and the last one off.

I was promoted to varsity in my junior year, but Don Shannon, our outstanding senior quarterback, was starting. In our third game, he broke his leg and missed the remainder of the season. His misfortune was my opportunity.

Because Lanier was the only public high school in Montgomery, Coach Moseley had an abundance of talented young athletes. Montgomery's residents followed high school football with a passion, and they were in for a treat. We were undefeated in my junior year. Surely my individual awards and our team success would please Dad. It may have, but he stepped up his critiques, second-guessing play calling and criticizing poor passes. I wanted to improve as badly as he wanted me to, but I needed a mentor. Coach Moseley led me to him.

In the summer of 1951, prior to my senior year at Lanier, the coach made arrangements for me to receive specialized instruction from Babe Parilli, Kentucky's All-American quarterback, who was preparing for his senior season. I had seen Babe play against Mississippi State in his junior year and knew he was a magician with the ball.

In three weeks, he taught me the fundamentals of playing quarterback. He also boosted my confidence. When I first arrived, I was so nervous I dropped my food tray while walking through the cafeteria line. By the end of our session, I visualized myself in a starring role for Bear Bryant's Kentucky Wildcats. When I returned to Montgomery, I taped pictures of Babe all over my bedroom.

As I entered my senior year of high school, football was my only love. But secure as I was about my quarterbacking abilities, I was painfully shy with girls. My buddies and I often went to the dances stag; we didn't usually have the courage to ask anyone.

The first girl who really caught my eye was Cherry Louise Morton, a beautiful brunette. For weeks I wanted to ask her out, but she was dating a guy from a wealthy family and I thought she might turn me down. One day at school I had my friend Nick Germanos ask Cherry if she would go out with me. "If he wants a date," she answered, "he will have to ask me himself." I finally mustered enough courage, and she accepted, although she later claimed she never saw my face, I was so busy staring at the floor and shuffling my feet.

On one of our first dates, I took her to the drive-in. I was a nervous wreck—I kept thinking, "Don't do or say anything stupid, or she'll never date you again." In all those high-stakes football games I hadn't once felt butterflies like this. Cherry, on the other hand, was as calm as I was fidgety. Too calm. When I returned from the popcorn stand, I saw her leaning slightly toward my seat, eyes closed, lips relaxed. I put my arm around her in anticipation of our first kiss, but my hopes were dashed when I discovered that she was sound asleep. This was just the boost of confidence I needed. I drove her home and, though she insisted she had a wonderful time, I was convinced I had flopped. The next morning in school she explained that for the first time, she had felt completely at ease with her date. I must have done something right— we dated steadily our entire senior year.

Remaining close to Cherry became the overriding factor in my choice of a university. She had committed herself to attending Auburn, located in eastern Alabama. My dream of playing for Bear Bryant and Kentucky began to fade. After my senior year, I was selected to the all-state team and recruited by every Southeastern Conference school except

Tennessee. Kentucky pushed for me heavily, and Nick Germanos, Bobby Barnes, and I visited the campus in Lexington one weekend while the Wildcats were hosting Tennessee. His team lost, but Coach Bryant was gracious and warm during our meeting the next morning. I was convinced that he would be as successful as Kentucky's Adolph Rupp was in basketball.

However, it was obvious my dad preferred watching me play for Alabama, since several times during the train ride to and from Lexington he remarked how far away it seemed. Additionally, I was afraid I would lose Cherry if I attended Kentucky. So I chose the University of Alabama. The Crimson Tide had a great football tradition, and the Tuscaloosa campus was only 130 miles from Auburn. It was one of the best decisions I ever made.

# CHAPTER

# 2

*"Attempt the end, and never stand to doubt;
Nothing's so hard but search will find it out."*

—Richard Lovelace

Every kid growing up in Alabama admired the Tide's legendary players—receiver Don Hutson, lineman Fred Sington, tailback Dixie Howell, passer Harry Gilmer. I was thrilled when Joe Kilgrow, an All-American halfback in the 1930s, and Bubba Nesbit, a star fullback from the same era, invited me to visit the Tuscaloosa campus after our senior football season the fall of my senior year. They introduced me to Frank Thomas, the legendary former coach who helped establish Alabama as a perennial power. He led the Tide to five Rose Bowl victories, four Southeastern Conference titles, and two national championships during his fifteen-year tenure. What I remember most about Coach Thomas, however, was his emphasis on academics. "Son," he said, "you'll enjoy playing football here. But you'll also get a good education." I accepted Alabama's scholarship offer a few weeks later.

I spent my spring semester at Sidney Lanier playing varsity baseball and earning some money for Alabama. Coach Moseley helped by giving me a job repairing the football field. My responsibility was to reseed the middle of the field where the ground was bare. After completing one patch, I yelled across the field, "Coach, I need some more manure."

When I looked up, I noticed my English teacher standing on the sidelines with Coach Moseley. In a loud stage whisper, she said, "Bill, can't you get him to say 'fertilizer'?"

He responded, "Miss Persons, do you have any idea how long it took us to get him to say 'manure'?"

That fall I joined a Crimson Tide team that was touted as one of the strongest in the nation. My transition from high school to college was made easier by the presence of Nick Germanos and Bobby Barnes, high school buddies who also accepted scholarships to play at Alabama. We were excited because the collegiate rules had recently been changed, making freshmen eligible to play varsity football.

Red Drew, who succeeded Thomas in 1947, all but abandoned the Notre Dame box offense and relied primarily on the split T formation. This scheme required a quarterback to be equally adept at running and passing. I was not an accomplished runner, however, and presented no immediate threat to Clell Hobson and Bobby Wilson, Alabama's returning quarterbacks. Our coaches decided to carry three quarterbacks on the varsity roster, which meant I had to battle Albert Elmore, a fellow freshman, for the third spot. Albert was a strong and talented athlete, but I managed to edge him out. My goal from that point on was to get enough playing time to earn a letter.

Our team, led by the strong running of All-American Bobby Marlow and Corky Tharp, compiled a record of 9 wins and 2 losses. On New Year's Day, we defeated Syracuse in the Orange Bowl by the score of 61–6. It was the most one-sided victory in major Bowl competition history, and I had a small part in the establishment of another record that day. I entered the game in the fourth quarter with instructions to throw the ball to receiver Joe Curtis. He was within one catch of setting an Orange Bowl record for pass receptions. After dropping

the first three passes, Curtis was subjected to persistent badg-
ering from our other receiver, Joe "Muleshoe" Cummings,
who shouted, "Hang on to it, you dummy!" My touchdown
pass to Curtis ended the scoring and silenced the Mule.

That spring, I faced a dilemma. I was still interested in
playing baseball and believed that I could make the varsity
team. Mom's brother-in-law, Hilton Battle, was as big a baseball fan as Dad, and they took turns calling me to make sure
I tried out. However, I wanted to spend more time with
Cherry and knew that if I played baseball, I wouldn't see her
very often. It was a close call, but the pretty brunette won.
Dad respected my decision, but my uncle was flabbergasted.
He called me and said "I can't believe you're going to drive
to Auburn to see some girl. You'd be better off chasing fly
balls!" My decision stuck.

In my sophomore year, I became Alabama's starting quarterback and shared the punting with halfback Bobby Luna.
My average of 41.4 yards per kick was second in the nation
behind Zeke Bratkowski of Georgia. I had additional motivation to kick them long and high—a recent rule change
prohibited unlimited substitution, and I was starting at defensive back.

Our record of 6-2-3 led to an appearance in the Cotton
Bowl, where we played Rice, who featured All-American
running back Dicky Moegle. My two interceptions did little
to stop the Owls, as they manhandled us 28–3.

The game's most memorable play, however, was made
by one of our running backs. Unfortunately, it occurred when
our defense was on the field. With Rice in the hole at their
own 5-yard line, Moegle swept right. I moved up to make
the tackle, but one of their blockers wiped me out. As I
scrambled to my feet, I saw Moegle sprinting down the sideline on a 95-yard jaunt. Suddenly, as he crossed midfield,
he was slammed to the turf by an Alabama player who had
run onto the field from our bench. It was Tommy Lewis, our
fullback. It had been a frustrating day for us offensively, and
Tommy just lost his head. Rice was awarded a touchdown;
Tommy received notoriety and an appearance on The Ed

*Sullivan Show.* Years later, Tommy, who had become an insurance executive, volunteered as an assistant coach at Huntsville High School. During a game against Sidney Lanier, a Lanier running back began streaking down the Huntsville sideline toward an uncontested touchdown. As he passed the 50-yard line, a kid from the Huntsville bench ran onto the field and tackled him. Coincidentally, he was wearing number 42, the same one Tommy had worn at Alabama.

When Tommy and I talked about the incident, he said, "Bart, for the first time in my life, I knew exactly how to console someone."

"Tommy," I replied, "you coached the boy well."

The Cotton Bowl defeat was disappointing, but I looked forward to two more seasons as Alabama's starting quarterback. I was also deeply in love.

Cherry and I had been dating three years. After attending Auburn her freshman year, she moved to Jackson, Mississippi, where her parents were then living. Whenever time permitted, I borrowed Bobby Barnes's slick new Mercury coupe to visit her; Bobby was stuck with my '39 Ford.

During those trips, Cherry and I often discussed the possibility of getting married. Our greatest fear had nothing to do with our relationship; rather, we knew that college football coaches frowned upon marriage and often rescinded scholarships of players who lost sight of the fact that football was supposed to come first.

One day in early May 1954, Cherry drove to see me in Tuscaloosa. On the spur of the moment, we decided to elope. We drove to Columbus, Mississippi, and were married in a short ceremony. Nick Germanos, who helped me get my first date with Cherry, was our witness. Following the ceremony, I drove Cherry to her parents' home while Nick returned in sworn secrecy to Tuscaloosa. There was no honeymoon.

I returned to school that summer without Cherry. She went to work as a typist for the L. M. Berry Company in Jackson. We didn't see each other again until late July. With the exception of Nick, no one knew we were married until I wrote Cherry a letter addressed to "Mrs. Bart Starr." Her mother noticed the name and asked Cherry, "Isn't this some-what presumptuous? You'd think the boy was married to you."

With tear-filled eyes, Cherry replied, "Well, he is."

Although Cherry's parents were thrilled, my mother was somewhat less than ecstatic. After I told my parents we were married, Mom called one day and suggested that Cherry and I drive to Montgomery to meet with our minister. We assumed she wanted us to receive some marriage counseling. When we arrived at the church, Mom was waiting with Dad and the minister. She said, "I want everyone to know that I'm going to have this marriage annulled if I have to take it all the way to the Supreme Court!"

Dad was more supportive but wanted me to concentrate on football and getting my degree; both of them wondered how a college athlete could support a wife. As Cherry and I moved into our small apartment, complete with a two-foot weed growing through the floorboards in the living room and a $15 bedroom suite, my parents had no way of knowing that I would be the one needing most of the support during the next two years.

While punting in a workout that summer before my junior year, I noticed a sharp pain in my lower back. Instead of stopping, I continued kicking. The next morning, I couldn't raise my leg above my waist. Like a fool, I kept trying to kick the ball when I should have been resting an injury. As it turned out, I suffered a severe back strain that would threaten to end my career and flare up intermittently for years.

When Alabama reported to fall practice, I was in traction, and remained there for several days. As I lay in the hospital bed, unable to even sit up, I wondered whether I could ever take another snap. Fortunately, I did recover, but saw only brief action in the last month. The Tide's lone bright spot that year was the play of Albert Elmore at quarterback. The team's 4-5-2 season was a disappointment; mine was a wash-out. Red Drew was replaced as head coach by J. B. Whitworth of Oklahoma A&M (now called Oklahoma State). I felt badly for Coach Drew but hoped that this change might turn my luck around.

Whitworth arrived with a commitment to clean house. With the exception of two seniors, he elected to field an entirely new lineup. He also installed the offensive system perfected by Oklahoma, college football's dominant power. He prefaced nearly every statement with "This is what they're doing at Oklahoma." What they were doing at Oklahoma was utilizing a split T offense that emphasized a quarterback's running rather than throwing ability. I quickly realized I would not be starting in the fall.

I was psychologically demoralized and didn't fare much better physically. That fall, I severely sprained an ankle and could no longer punt. My senior year was a disaster. I sat on the bench while Alabama lost ten straight games. For years it upset me when people said, "You played on the 1955 team that lost all its games."

Despite my limited playing time during my junior and senior years, I retained ambitions to pursue a career in professional football. My back problems were alleviated by a chiropractor, Dr. John Robinson, in Tuscaloosa; a more serious challenge was attracting the attention of NFL scouts. After two years of misfortune, however, my luck finally changed with the help of Johnny Dee.

Coach Dee, who arrived at Alabama the same year I did, successfully turned around Alabama's basketball program, leading them to a conference championship in his fourth year. I admired his aggressive coaching style and would often watch practice on my idle winter afternoons. He also assisted the football coaches by working with the punters and scouting future opponents. We became good friends during my sophomore year.

After my last game at Alabama, I visited Johnny in his office to discuss my future in professional football. He said, "The first thing we must do is get you in the Blue-Gray game. It shouldn't be too hard for a kid from Alabama."

That prospect excited me because the game has always been played in the Montgomery Crampton Bowl, where we played our high school games. I wanted the opportunity to prove to the people in my hometown that I could still perform. More important, the pro scouts would evaluate participating athletes.

Charley Winner, an assistant coach for the Baltimore Colts, approached me after practice one day and asked, "Can you play defense?"

"Coach," I answered, "I'll play anywhere. I just want a chance." I was smart and aggressive enough to play safety. I was also a sure tackler, but I had to be because of my lack of speed.

Paul Dietzel of LSU was the head coach of the Gray squad. Four years earlier, as an assistant at Kentucky, Bear Bryant assigned him to recruit me to that school. As I sat on the bench in front of my hometown friends, I couldn't help but believe he was holding my decision to play for Alabama against me. The only other quarterback on the Gray squad, Bob Hardy of Kentucky, played virtually the entire game despite having a sore arm.

I was bitter and embarrassed. I cried in frustration after the game. My future in football looked bleak. After I returned to school, however, Coach Dee said, "I'm going to call someone in the NFL for you. I think you can play."

I responded, "I know I can . . . if I get the opportunity."

Johnny knew Jack Vainisi, the director of player personnel for the Green Bay Packers, and Lou Rymkus, a Packer assistant coach. He called Vainisi to recommend me as a prospect. Vainisi told Johnny, "Rymkus will be down that way. He'll take a look at Starr."

In January 1956 the NFL conducted its draft of college seniors. The next morning, the Packers notified me that I had been selected in the seventeenth round. I was the one hundred and ninety-ninth player chosen—and elated.

I was somewhat familiar with the Packers because the Green Bay–Chicago games were televised in Alabama. Hamilton of the Canadian League also pursued me, but I could not picture myself playing in ice and snow. My thoughts turned to Green Bay.

Shortly after the draft, Ray "Scooter" McLean, a Packer assistant coach, traveled to Tuscaloosa to sign me. I was offered $6,500, which was less than Hamilton's bid. I asked for $7,500, intending to apply the extra $1,000 toward some unpaid medical bills incurred when Cherry suffered a miscarriage, and McLean telephoned the Packers for approval. I signed the contract thinking I would be paid $7,500 for my rookie season. However, the $1,000 I received on signing was not a bonus but rather an advance against my salary, which remained $6,500.

In the spring of 1956, I worked at a number of odd jobs while studying to complete my final semester. On graduation day, I received my diploma and the air force ROTC commission. When Dad saluted me, I returned it and handed him the traditional dollar for a first salute. As he looked at my lieutenant's bars, he smiled and said, "You might outrank me, but I'm still the boss." He topped it off with a big bear hug.

In preparation for the transition to professional football, I embarked on a rigorous program to rebuild my confidence as a passer. Johnny Dee helped again by securing three footballs for me, something the football coaches had been unwilling to do. Cherry and I moved in with her parents, Ed and Opal Hall, in Jackson. I built an A-frame in their yard, and every day for a month I threw footballs through a tire I'd suspended from it. The three footballs became so battered and swollen they began to resemble the old-fashioned "round" footballs from the 1930s.

Cherry was there with me, retrieving errant passes and providing constant encouragement. At times, it seemed like she had as much enthusiasm as I. One day I asked her how she could possibly be running around with a smile on her face. She replied, "I checked my weight this morning and discovered that I had lost five pounds!" I was convinced those workouts would enable me to make the Packer roster as a rookie. I was ready for the National Football League.

# CHAPTER

# 3

I arrived in Green Bay for the first time on a cloudy day in late June 1956. Unlike the sweltering Alabama summer, the weather there was cool and damp. Sweaters were necessary. "If it's this cold in June," I thought, "what's it going to be like in December?"

At the time, the Packers held their preseason training in Stevens Point, Wisconsin. Although camp did not begin for another week, several rookies were brought to Green Bay to work out for the college all-star game, which was to be held in a few weeks.

We were met at the airport by Tom Miller, a member of the Packers' front-office staff, and driven to the Northland Hotel, in the middle of town. Meals were provided directly across the street at the YMCA cafeteria. We worked out at nearby East High School, which was also where the Packers played during the regular season.

I was shocked when I saw the Packer locker room—thirty-three lockers jammed together in an area no larger than Dad's garage in Montgomery. The Packer offices were located in a red-brick, two-story building next to the Downtowner Motel. The space was so small that the coaches had to enter their offices through a side door.

Our gear was issued to us from a shed near the practice field. The condition of the equipment was far below what I had expected. Gary Knafelc, a wide receiver, recalled, "I had better stuff than that in high school." In fact, while in training camp his rookie year, Gary had his dad send him the pads he used in the college all-star game. He wore them the entire season.

The training room was equipped with a whirlpool that was nothing more than a large bathtub with a rusty pipe. The makeshift Jacuzzi occupied nearly half of the small room. Prior to practice, players waited in line outside the door to be taped.

Nonetheless, the inconveniences failed to diminish my exhilaration over the opportunity to play in the National Football League. I was thrilled by the challenge of proving myself against athletes who were far more talented than those I competed with in college.

After four days of practice and an introduction to the Packers' offensive system, three of the rookies, running back Jack Losch and offensive tackles Forrest Gregg and Bob Skoronski, left for Chicago to play in the college all-star game. While they prepared to face the defending NFL champion Cleveland Browns, the rest of us moved on to the Packers' training camp in Stevens Point, a small town in the heart of Wisconsin's dairyland.

Green Bay, boasting a population of approximately fifty thousand, was a big city by comparison. Following his flight from Chicago to join the team after the all-star game, Bob Skoronski said, "I thought Green Bay was the end of the world. Then on the way up here, I wondered, 'Where the hell are we going now?' There isn't even a building next to the runway at the damn airport. What if someone had to take a leak?"

On my arrival in Stevens Point, I quickly realized that although it was a small community, it was unique, and the people there were very special. I also realized that the Packers were giving me little chance to make the roster. When jerseys were passed out, I was given 42, a number usually reserved for backs and receivers. My earliest bubble-gum card shows me wearing that number. It is not worth a 1952 Mickey Mantle, but it may be a collector's item nonetheless.

The head coach of the Packers was Lisle Blackbourn. He was well known in Wisconsin, having coached Marquette University in Milwaukee before accepting Green Bay's offer in 1954. Coach Blackbourn made it clear from the beginning that only two quarterbacks would make the final squad in 1956—and one of those was Tobin Rote, the previous year's all-pro field general. Four competed for the backup spot— two other rookies besides me, and Paul Held, the previous year's reserve quarterback.

I was clearly the least physically gifted. I was also the best prepared. Without the hard work I had put in on Ed Hall's lawn in Jackson, I would have had little chance against those three superior athletes.

My performance in our first two scrimmages convinced the coaches that I should play in the preseason games. Although I lacked professional experience, I had both confidence in myself and an excellent role model in Tobin. He was an ideal physical specimen, six feet three, 210 pounds, and had a competitive desire to match. In fact, I might have played more during the preseason had Tobin not been such a fighter. I remember entering games after he had been knocked out by a blind-side shot, only to see him run back to the huddle one play later. But if Tobin's play kept me from participating much during my first year, his advice helped me become a more accomplished quarterback. He told me, "Your arm isn't strong enough and you won't last long if you don't improve. You don't have to throw the ball seventy-five yards, but you must put enough zip on it to make the defense respect you. If they don't, the opposing defensive backs will eat your receivers alive."

Although conditioning was emphasized, strength and weight-lifting programs were virtually unheard of for football players in those days, especially for quarterbacks. Nonetheless, realizing Tobin was right, I began a program to further develop my arm strength using conventional means . . . my arm and a football.

Tobin was not only the team's leader, he was occasionally the boss. I was astonished during a preseason game when I saw the chain of command flow from Tobin to Coach Blackbourn. Following a play, Blackbourn attempted to make a substitution, but Tobin didn't want that particular player in the game, and sent him back to the sideline. Tobin was hardly the only talented or charismatic player on that team, however.

Howie Ferguson was a rugged running back who gained 859 yards in a twelve-game season the previous year. Fred Cone was a versatile athlete—a hard-charging fullback and accurate placekicker. Al Carmichael was an outstanding running back and kickoff-return man, whose NFL-record 106-yard return may never be broken. Our incumbent center, Jim Ringo, was an all-pro. He also possessed a unique sense of humor.

On my first day of practice, Tobin asked me to fill in for him as the holder during a postpractice field-goal drill. Ringo was snapping the balls. The first snap sailed yards to my left, and I fell over trying to grab it. The second snap was six feet over my head, the third in the dirt. I shook my head in disgust, wondering, "What the hell is going on here?" Ringo was supposed to be one of the best centers in the league. After a few more errant snaps, he turned around with a huge grin on his face and said slyly, "Starr, I'll never forget that damn Orange Bowl game." He was the center on the Syracuse team Alabama had humiliated.

Perhaps our most impressive player other than Tobin was receiver Bill Howton. During one of our scrimmages, I threw a bull's-eye that hit him as he crossed the end zone. He dropped it. I was not about to chew out a man who was on the verge of becoming the Packers' all-time leading receiver.

He came back to the huddle and said, "Rook, that was a fine pass. I'll never drop another one." And he didn't. Bill's attitude left an indelible impression on me and fortified my desire to succeed. His unwillingness to accept anything less than perfection exemplified the attitude of a true professional athlete.

The 1956 Packers were not lacking in defensive talent either. Linemen Dave "Hawg" Hanner and John Martinkovic, linebackers Roger Zatkoff, Bill Forester, Tom Bettis, and Deral Teteak, and safety Bobby Dillon were aggressive and productive players. Dillon was a consistent all-pro despite having sight in only one eye.

Although there was an abundance of talent, the Packers lacked coaching leadership and had become accustomed to losing. The team was dominated by a group of rugged, fun-loving guys who had the desire to win, but never let the outcome of a game affect their performances off the field.

One day Paul Held saw Martinkovic sitting on the trainer's table, stripped to his waist. Martinkovic was extremely hairy. Held grabbed a strip of athletic tape, and as he approached Martinkovic, he pretended to stumble, reached out, and slapped the tape across Martinkovic's chest. He said, "Oops, sorry," and yanked the tape—and hair—back. Martinkovic shifted the chaw of tobacco in his cheek, let fly, and hit Held with a stream of tobacco juice right between the eyes.

A few days later, two of Martinkovic's fellow defensive linemen, Jerry Helluin and Dick "The Bruiser" Afflis, entered into a beer-can-crushing contest. Style usually determined the winner—they crushed cans behind their backs, on their heads, under their arms. Finally, The Bruiser mashed one against his nose. Blood streamed down his face as he asked, "What do you think of that?"

Helluin replied, "You win."

At breakfast one morning, Fred Cone poured the contents of a salt shaker into a glass of orange juice and set the glass on the table in front of an empty seat. Shortly thereafter, Coach Blackbourn came along and sat down in that place.

Most people sip orange juice. He tossed it down in one gulp, and his eyes crossed as he reached for his throat with his left hand.

Ringo was determined to keep Al Carmichael in his room and make him miss a team meeting—automatic fine, of course—just as a prank. While Al was asleep, he taped the door shut by wrapping adhesive tape around the doorknob and running the tape across the hall to another doorknob. While the rest of the team was in the meeting, Al was trapped in his room . . . and fined.

The high jinks of the veterans provided amusement in the middle of an otherwise emotionally draining experience. I still dwelled too long on my mistakes and worried that I might not make the team. My confidence improved dramatically a few weeks later when the coaches narrowed the list of quarterback contenders from five to three—Tobin, Paul, and me. I called Cherry, who had remained in Jackson, and told her, "Pack the car and head this way."

Her parents were extremely supportive—her mother accompanied her on the drive in a brand-new Chevy given to me by her father. He told me, "You can repay me if you make the team. If you don't, consider it a gift." No son-in-law ever received more love than the amount Cherry's folks showered on me.

Cherry was in for quite a shock when she arrived. She lived in a dry state and had never tried an alcoholic beverage. When she entered Green Bay on Broadway Avenue, she counted twenty-three taverns in the first mile. Milwaukee produced most of the beer in the country and Green Bay consumed it.

Despite Cherry's initial reaction, she was quickly won over by the warmth of Green Bay's residents. The first evening she was in Green Bay, Jerry Atkinson, the president of H. C. Prange Company, introduced himself to her at a restaurant on the top floor of the store, where Cherry and her mom were eating dinner. Jerry, a member of the Packers' board of directors, and later vice-president of the team's executive committee, became one of our closest friends. He was one of my staunchest supporters throughout my career as a player and as a coach.

Paul Held was released following our final preseason game. After we learned that I had made the team, Cherry and I moved into a house on Hickory Hill Drive, in a pleasant middle-class neighborhood on the west side of town. The house had been for sale but Cherry somehow managed to talk the owners into renting it to us until the season ended.

I saw limited action in my first year. I started only one game, against San Francisco, when Tobin was hindered by a shoulder strain. My season totals were forty-four attempts, twenty-four completions, two touchdowns, and three interceptions. Our team stumbled to a record of 4-8.

One bright spot, in an otherwise dismal season, occurred when Dad and Mom visited Green Bay for our game against the 49ers. Following the game I thought football would be the first and foremost subject on Dad's mind. However, to my astonishment, he was persistent only in taking a ride through the neighboring countryside to see some of Wisconsin's fertile farmland. As we were driving down a country road, Dad asked me to stop the car. He got out and walked the short distance to a farmer's field, where he bent over and grasped a handful of dirt. Holding his arm in the air, he slowly opened his fingers and admired the rich soil as it drifted to the ground. When he returned to the car, he said, "Son, the good Lord knew what he was doing. If he had blessed us with such fine soil in Alabama, there wouldn't be anyone living up here."

A month after the season ended, concern over my future as a pro quarterback reached its peak. On January 3, 1957, I was called to active duty in the air force, based on my ROTC commission, and assigned to the Eglin base near Panama City, Florida. Service football was popular at the time and helped take everyone's mind off the Korean War. Zeke Bratkowski, my collegiate adversary at Georgia, was finishing his two-year hitch at Eglin, and the commanding general needed a new quarterback. My physical, however, revealed that I still had a back problem.

The orthopedic physician who examined me, knowing I had been brought to Eglin to play football, deferred the final decision on my fitness for duty to the base commander. When the general in command returned from leave two weeks later, he refused to sign the medical waiver that would have been necessary for me to remain on active duty. I stayed at Eglin for six more weeks prior to receiving a medical discharge.

I was apprehensive about the call home to tell Dad that I had been discharged from the air force. When I reached him, he said laughingly, "Son, I didn't think you would make a career of it, but don't you think two months is a little ridiculous?"

I was delighted to be back in Green Bay by early May. The citizens made me feel as though I had lived there all my life. Cherry and I were befriended by Eddie Ginsberg, owner of an auto-salvage company. He and his wife, Louise, offered to share their home on Burns Avenue with us, and we lived in their upstairs apartment for two years. We looked forward to raising our family in a safe, quiet town with traditional values. Despite the severe winters, northeastern Wisconsin was a recreational paradise.

For Nate Borden, however, Green Bay was something less than a second home. Nate was drafted by the Packers in 1955 from Indiana University and was the only black player on the team when I arrived. Unable to find suitable housing within the city, he attempted to move into a motel just outside of town that had been made available to the Packers in the fall.

There he encountered the unkindest cut of all—his teammates, many of whom were from the South, rejected him. They told the motel manager in no uncertain terms that they would leave if Nate was allowed to rent a room. Finally, in desperation, Nate and his family moved into what was little more than a shanty.

Having grown up in Montgomery, I was used to seeing racial bias and hatred, but I couldn't believe that Nate's own teammates had turned their backs on him. Cherry and I decided to call Nate and ask him to join us for dinner one

evening. Although we knew it was impossible to truly em-
pathize with what Nate was going through, we felt badly for
him and wanted him to know we and a local family cared.
From that day on, Nate and his family were frequent visitors
to the Ginsberg residence.

My chances to be the starting quarterback of the Packers
improved dramatically on the day before I was due to report
to training camp in July 1957. Tobin Rote, Fred Cone, and I
went out to play a round of golf and relax before our work
began. The first hole at Town and Country Golf Club was a
short par 4, about 260 yards, and Tobin had a 2-iron in his
hand.

I had my driver out and asked Tobin, "Why are you hit-
ting a two-iron?"

He said, "I don't want to knock it over the green."

As he prepared to hit, Jack Vainisi ran up to the tee and
said to Tobin, "You've just been traded to the Detroit Lions."

Tobin was livid. He knew he would be joining a team
that had an established quarterback in Bobby Layne. In addition, he was settled in Green Bay and comfortable there,
despite playing on a losing team. For a moment I thought
he was going to smash his 2-iron over Jack's head. Fred and
I offered to cancel the game, but Tobin insisted we play. He
put his 2-iron back in his bag, yanked out his driver, and
nailed his tee shot off a house 30 yards beyond the green.
His ball came to rest against a garden hose.

As we approached it, Tobin turned to Fred and asked,
"How about some relief?"

Fred decided to jab his now ex-teammate and said, "Nope.
In Detroit they play summer rules."

The move to Detroit turned out to be a good one for Tobin.
He and Bobby shared playing time that season until Layne
broke an ankle in the second-to-last game. Detroit finished
the season with two victories and tied San Francisco to force
a playoff game for the Western Conference title. In that game,
the Lions trailed the 49ers 27–7 in the third quarter, until
Tobin led a rally that ended in a 31–27 Detroit victory.

The following week, in the 1957 NFL championship game,

Tobin threw four touchdown passes, leading the Lions to a 59–14 rout over the Cleveland Browns.

The Packers' decision to trade Tobin provided me with a unique opportunity but also put me in an awkward position. I would be competing with Babe Parilli for the starting-quarterback spot.

During the off-season, Babe had been acquired from the Cleveland Browns. While playing golf with Tobin and Fred, I also found it difficult to concentrate on my game. I kept thinking back to the summer of 1951, when Babe worked as hard as I did to improve my quarterbacking skills. I knew then that I could never repay him, and now I had to compete against him. How would he react when I said hello and shook his hand for the first time since saying good-bye six years before?

The following morning, Cherry drove me to the locker room for the team's opening-day meeting. As I entered the it, Babe was just inside, chatting with another player. He turned to me, smiled, and said, "Hello, Bart."

"Hi, Babe. It's good to see you again."

As we walked toward our lockers, he stopped and said, "Bart, I know you probably feel as uncomfortable about this situation as I do. When we worked together in Lexington, I said you could be a great quarterback. Prove it to me. Let's push each other and have some fun." Babe had not changed a bit—he was still interested in my success, and he still put me at ease.

Although we had an amicable relationship, the Packers put it to the test by making us roommates. Ideally, I would have preferred rooming with a defensive player so I could relax and obtain a different perspective. Babe and I handled the situation diplomatically, however, and remained good friends.

Our competition during training camp was too close to call, but I got the starting assignment for our 1957 season opener. We celebrated the dedication of Lambeau Field— named for the Packers' founder, Curly Lambeau—with a stirring 21–17 victory over the Chicago Bears, the defending Western Conference champs.

We next hosted the Detroit Lions, and I looked forward to another exciting weekend. I received more than I could handle.

On Saturday morning, Cherry went into labor. As I drove her to Bellin Hospital, I was thankful she was going to have our baby the day before the game. By Saturday evening, however, she was still having contractions. I stayed up with her all night while her pain and my agitation became worse. At eight o'clock Sunday morning, I left the hospital to attend the pregame meal. Her obstetrician told me, "We'll do our best. Your wife and baby will pull through." I played one of the worst games of my life and contributed substantially to our defeat. Fortunately, Cherry gave birth to a healthy Bryan Bartlett Starr, Jr., later that evening.

The sight of our first child was indescribable. Although disappointed over being unable to witness the birth, I was grateful that mom and son survived the ordeal.

We didn't have much else to cheer about that year. Babe and I rotated at quarterback, but neither was particularly effective. We finished the season with a record of 3-9, and Coach Blackbourn was released. He was a good teacher and a good man, respected by his players. His coaching experience at Marquette University, however, did not adequately prepare him for professional competition. His successor was Scooter McLean, who had been an assistant coach at Green Bay for several years.

If our 1957 record was disappointing, our 1958 performance was embarrassing. We won only one game, and lost a contest to Baltimore 56–0. Scooter McLean's friendly and relaxed demeanor would have been perfect for some teams, but not ours. Discipline and morale were at an all-time low.

# CHAPTER

## 4

*"It is time for a new generation of
leadership, to cope with new problems
and new opportunities. For there is a
new world to be won."*

—JOHN FITZGERALD KENNEDY

On February 4, 1959, the Green Bay Packers appointed Vince
Lombardi as their head coach and general manager. When I
picked up a Green Bay *Press-Gazette* to learn more about
him, I glanced at an accompanying photo and realized I had
seen him before. Something seemed wrong, however, when
the article referred to him as the former offensive coordinator
of the New York Giants.

During a preseason game in 1958, the Giants hosted the
Packers at Fenway Park in Boston. As I jogged toward our
bench following a touchdown, I heard a man screaming at
the top of his lungs from the sideline. I looked at the Giants'
bench and saw a stout, burly man with graying hair who
seemed to be all mouth as he continued to yell at the New
York defensive players for allowing us to score. I had no
idea who he was, but assumed he was a defensive coach.

While a student at Fordham University—a collegiate
football power in the 1930's—Lombardi was a 180-pound
guard on the "Seven Blocks of Granite." Several members

of that unit went on to play professional football. Lombardi, however, lacked size and began a teaching career. He taught physics and Latin at St. Cecilia High School in Englewood, New Jersey, before returning to Fordham to coach football. In 1947, Colonel Earl "Red" Blaik hired Lombardi as an assistant coach at the U.S. Military Academy. Blaik, one of the game's legendary coaches, had already led Army to national prominence in the Glenn Davis–Doc Blanchard era.

Colonel Blaik recalled, "I hired him more for his mind than his coaching experience. The fact that he taught Latin and physics led me to believe he could be an excellent instructor on the football field as well. He was also extremely enthusiastic. The first day of spring practice, he was working with the defensive line, when I called him over to discuss some defensive alignments. As we talked, he kept glancing back at his players. Suddenly, he turned and ran toward them, yelling, 'What the hell's going on out here!' As he continued his tirade, I said, 'Vince . . . VINCE!' He stopped and I calmly told him, 'Vince, we don't coach that way at West Point.' I never had to remind him.

"I guess he went back to yelling when he was hired by the Packers."

Actually, Lombardi resumed his hollering when he joined the Giants as an assistant coach in 1954. Their owner, Wellington Mara, attended Fordham with Lombardi and was aware of his coaching ability. Head Coach Jim Lee Howell also believed Lombardi would be an excellent addition to his staff.

Two years later, with Lombardi coaching the Giants' offense and Tom Landry the defense, New York won the NFL championship. Lombardi built the New York offense around the varied talents of halfback Frank Gifford and gained a reputation for possessing one of the brightest offensive minds in professional football.

Although Lombardi was instrumental in the Giants' success, he was not content as an assistant. He applied for several head coaching positions at major universities, until the Packers hired him as their head coach and general manager.

My first meeting with Coach Lombardi occurred in the

spring of 1959, when he assembled the team's quarterbacks in Green Bay. I distinctly recall the abrupt manner with which he greeted us—"Good morning, I'm Vince Lombardi." With the pleasantries out of the way, he immediately began to discuss how he would instill renewed pride in the Packer organization.

During the course of a three-hour meeting, I became increasingly impressed with his knowledge of the game and his ability to convey it. He could diagram a play without losing eye contact. When we broke for lunch, I called Cherry and said, "Things are going to change around here."

Lombardi was consistent and disciplined in his approach; the word "discipline" was prominent in his vocabulary. He left no doubt what he expected and, more important, explained why. He took great pride in coaching, often describing it as the epitomy of teaching. Lombardi was in fact a great teacher, whose lessons extended far beyond the playing field. He knew that no one could ever be perfect, but believed that through chasing perfection, we could achieve excellence. He emphasized the need to focus all attention on one objective in order to succeed, and referred to it as "singleness of purpose." As a result, Lombardi detested any *outside* activity of a player that might distract him from concentrating on football whether it was a player's business interests or haggling over game tickets for friends and relatives.

Winning to Lombardi was neither everything nor the only thing. He was more interested in seeing us make the effort to be our best. If we did, he knew that winning would usually take care of itself.

However, perhaps the greatest misconception regarding Lombardi resulted from Henry Jordan's classic comment: "He treated us all the same . . . like dogs." Actually, Lombardi was a master at varying his approach depending on the emotional makeup of a particular individual.

A perfect example of Lombardi's ability to read his players is illustrated by his treatment of two of our offensive linemen, Bob Skoronski and Jerry Kramer.

Bob, an offensive tackle from Indiana University, was one

of the brightest football players I have ever seen at any position. He possessed average size, six feet three and 245 pounds, good athletic ability, and remarkable intuition. He took tremendous pride in his work and was self-motivated. On the rare occasions when he missed an assignment or failed to execute his blocks, he knew it before anyone else.

When Lombardi first arrived, he criticized Bob unmercifully. Bob realized that Lombardi's personal comments were directed at the team, but he was sensitive to it. He didn't believe in motivation by fear. Eventually, however, Lombardi adjusted and motivated Bob by appealing to his reason.

Jerry Kramer, our right guard, was also an intelligent player, an outgoing, aggressive man who grew up in a small town in Idaho and loved to get physical during games, and one of Lombardi's favorite targets. Lombardi consistently challenged his ability, his toughness, his manhood.

Initially, Jerry detested Lombardi so much that he considered jumping to the American Football League. After three or four years, however, Jerry became one of Lombardi's most loyal players. He also became one of the best offensive linemen in pro football.

It is no secret that Lombardi was often extremely hard on a particular player or the entire team. His ability to select the most appropriate time to criticize was the factor that made his remarks so effective. During his first year, we lost a heartbreaker to a superior team in the final minutes. As we waited for his postgame entrance into the locker room, most of the players were dreading what would surely be his tirade. Instead, he calmly walked in and said, "Men, you have nothing to be ashamed of. I know you guys gave it your best shot and that's what's important. We will all be better off for it." The team quickly regrouped and went on to finish the season 7-5.

If Lombardi was surprisingly compassionate in defeat, he could be just as tough on us in victory, at least when our performance warranted it. After defeating the St. Louis Cardinals by a huge margin in a preseason game, we walked off the field laughing and slapping each other's backs. When we

entered the locker room, however, Lombardi was waiting
and quickly brought us back to earth. He said, "Our performance tonight was a disgrace. The only reason we won is
because the Cardinals were even worse! You didn't give a
damn about playing your best . . . you only cared about that
damn score." As he continued his fierce harangue, I thought
he must be crazy. When I viewed the game films the next
morning, I realized he was right.

On the rare occasion when Lombardi was wrong, he didn't
hesitate to admit it, except to me. During a training-camp
practice drill, I threw a pass that was tipped by a defensive
lineman and intercepted. Lombardi was infuriated. I ran over
to tackle the linebacker who intercepted the pass, but Lombardi jumped between us and screamed: "Damn you, don't
you understand we're working to cut down mistakes? Instead, you throw a lousy interception! Throw it away, eat it,
do anything, but not a turnover!"

As soon as practice was over, I went to see him in his
office. I said, "Coach, I've been with you for a year now,
working my butt off to be the leader you demand. That ball
was tipped. It wasn't a clean interception . . . those things
can happen."

"Bart, you're right," he replied.

"Coach, if you're going to blister me in front of the team,
at least have the guts to apologize in their presence as well.
I want them to know I have your respect."

He said softly, "OK." Seldom again did he berate me in
front of my teammates. Prior to our confrontation in his
office, I believe he tested me to see if I had enough character
to stand up to him. Lombardi never resented being challenged by a player he respected. After one particularly lack-
luster victory, he called us a bunch of dummies and
incompetents. Bob Skoronski jumped up and said, "Don't
put me in that class." Lombardi, realizing that Bob was one
of his most consistent performers, quickly changed the subject.

The fact that Lombardi was so demanding is not as important as the reason for his style. He believed that we would

play to our potential on Sunday if we were challenged during the week. He was right. Our practices were tougher than the games, but they also trained us to "do things right all the time."

Lombardi's reputation as tyrant on the practice field was only partially correct. During our first training camp under him, he implemented the infamous grass drills. Most of the players were unprepared for the rigorous nature and length of the drill. Dave Hanner, our defensive tackle, collapsed and was taken to the hospital, where he was treated for heat exhaustion and remained for two days. When Dave returned to training camp the next year we presented him with a certificate for two days' room and board at the hospital of his choice.

As difficult as practices were in training camp, especially when a guest coach such as Woody Hayes would attend, our regular-season practices were not physically taxing at all. Lombardi understood the value of fresh legs on Sunday and focused instead on preparing us emotionally and mentally.

Many coaches and business executives believe that an individual performs best when least secure. Lombardi certainly subscribed to this theory. He made it certain that every player knew he was only as good as his most recent performance.

Gary Knafelc's experience with Coach Lombardi indicates how intimidating the man could be. Before Lombardi joined Green Bay, Gary was playing flanker. The first week of training camp, however, Gary recalls Lombardi calling him aside and asking, "How much do you weigh?"

"About two twenty-five," answered Gary.

"You're going to play tight end," said Lombardi.

Jokingly, Gary responded, "Coach, I haven't hit anybody in five years."

Lombardi gave him a long, cold, impersonal look before asking, "Where would you like to go?"

Gary, who had recently purchased a new home in Green Bay, said, "I want to stay right here, Coach."

Gary immediately worked to improve his strength, and

he eventually became a very good player at a position where blocking ability was critical to the offense's success.

"I would bite, hold, do anything I could," said Gary about his experience playing tight end. "I feared Lombardi more than any defensive end or linebacker I ever played against. I only had to deal with those guys once or twice a year. I saw Lombardi every day."

Lombardi continued to intimidate Gary even after he left the Packers. In 1963, following his release from Green Bay, Gary joined the San Francisco 49ers for his final pro season. The Packers ended their season that year against the 49ers in San Francisco. Gary still made his home in Green Bay, and asked me if I would get permission from Coach Lombardi for him to fly back with us the next afternoon. Bold and brave, I suggested he ask Coach Lombardi's wife, Marie.

When Gary called her, she said, "Why don't you talk to Vince?" Gary confessed he was still scared to death of Lombardi. Marie called back and said Vince would be happy to take him back to Green Bay with the team.

At the San Francisco airport following the game, several players, including Gary, were standing at a bar watching a football game on television. Lombardi prohibited players from sitting or standing at any bar. As the group's interest in the game heightened, Lombardi walked in and howled, "Get the hell outta here."

All of the players scattered, and right with them was Gary. Marie Lombardi grabbed him by the arm and said, "Gary, you don't have to leave. You're not with the team anymore."

"I'm still afraid of that man," he answered.

Gary was hardly the first player Lombardi intimidated, however. In fact, Lombardi made it perfectly clear that there would be only one boss during a confrontation with Bill Howton, our all-pro receiver and unofficial leader. When Lombardi arrived in Green Bay, Bill decided to pay him a visit to share his assessment of the team. We waited anxiously for Bill to emerge from their meeting. After about thirty minutes, he came out with a somber look on his face and said, "Well, I think you guys are in for a surprise this year." The next day we learned that Bill had been traded to Cleveland.

With Bill no longer around to catch any passes, Gary had an excellent season. He caught twenty-seven passes and scored four times. He also blocked like hell.

After the season, Gary decided he was due a substantial raise, so he had a secretary type up his offer. He went to great lengths to point out that he caught almost every pass thrown to him. He even claimed to have executed more blocks than anyone on the team, more than Jim Ringo, more than Forrest Gregg. He was confident as he walked into Lombardi's office and presented him the offer.

"Coach," he said, "as you can see, these numbers speak for themselves. I don't even want to have a discussion about the contract. I've earned what I'm asking for."

Lombardi looked at the paper for about a minute. Two minutes. Three. Gary began to feel somewhat uneasy.

Finally, Lombardi said, "You forgot to mention one very important fact."

"What's that, Coach?"

"You only played offense last year."

"What? I mean, Coach, what are you talking about?"

"You didn't play on the kickoff team, on the punt team, on extra points . . ."

Gary interrupted. "OK, Coach, what are you willing to pay me?"

Lombardi handed Gary a contract and he signed it immediately. "Hell, I was just glad he invited me back to training camp next year."

Lombardi was a terrific contract negotiator. He usually buttered us up, complimented us, built our self-esteem. Then he reminded us how fortunate we were to be playing for the Packers, how much playoff money we could make.

My most memorable negotiations with him occurred after the 1960 season. I decided to use reverse psychology. I knew that Lombardi would be expecting me to walk in and bashfully ask for a small raise. But I had a good season in 1960 and believed I deserved a major hike in pay.

I walked into his office assertively and said, "What are we going to do about my contract?"

Lombardi stared at me, saying nothing.

"This is what I want," I said, as I named a figure.

Still no response.

"Coach, I won't settle for anything less."

Lombardi finally laughed and said, "My God . . . I've created a monster! Bart, we're not that far apart. You win."

As excited as I was with the new contract, I was also wringing wet with perspiration.

Every successful coach has stressed the need to capitalize on an opponent's weaknesses. Lombardi, however, placed equal emphasis on attacking their strengths.

When we played the Chicago Bears, we keyed on Bill George, their all-pro middle linebacker. Because of his quickness, Bill was able to wait until I was into the cadence, then jump between our center and one of our guards as the ball was being snapped. His strategy was effective against most teams, but we looked forward to attacking him. Rather than try to prevent Bill from crossing the line of scrimmage, we let him do so and threw a quick pass to our tight end in the area he had vacated.

Lombardi's offensive system reflected his fundamental approach to the game. He installed a system of play calling that was simple yet effective. Before he arrived, we used the Clark Shaughnessy system, derived from the man who pioneered the T formation. When the quarterback called a play, he also spelled out the linemen's blocking assignments. Because defenses could shift from one alignment to another prior to the snap of the ball, linemen were forced to change the blocking assignments called by the quarterback in the huddle. Since the linemen were occasionally changing their assignments at the line of scrimmage, Lombardi stopped having the quarterback call them. "49-Bill-0-Grace-Ed" became "49." When Lombardi first implemented the change, one of our veteran linemen asked him during a meeting why. Lombardi snapped, "The quarterback has enough to worry about without calling your blocking assignment."

Because of his commitment to basic football, we were primarily a running team. Although he recognized the advantages of a strong passing attack, he knew its effectiveness was dependent upon the degree of respect our opponents had for our ability to run the ball. He also enjoyed capitalizing on the strength of our running game as much as I did. The first time I decided to pass in an obvious running situation occurred during a close game against the Lions. We were faced with a fourth and 1 at midfield, and I knew Detroit's defenders would be looking for a run by Jimmy Taylor, our fullback. Instead, I faked to Taylor and threw a strike to Max McGee for a touchdown. As I jogged off the field, Lombardi greeted me with a smile. "That was one hell of a call, Bart," he said. "I'm all for it, but you damn well better complete the pass."

Coach Lombardi was not without a sense of humor and enjoyed a good laugh. Prior to a Thanksgiving Day game in Detroit one year, several players learned that Coach Lombardi planned to go deer hunting with some friends that weekend. On Friday we held a team meeting to review the film. Following the meeting, while many of the players were assembled in the locker room, Zeke Bratkoski and I presented Coach Lombardi with a T-shirt that we had specially prepared for him. The T-shirt had ITALIAN HUNTING SHIRT printed across the front and a large target with a bull's-eye printed on the back. After a brief disappearance, Coach Lombardi returned wearing the shirt, and proceeded to strut around the locker room. When the laughter was beginning to subside, Zeke said, "Coach, we were going to get you a cap, too, but couldn't find one with antlers."

Perhaps the best example of Vince Lombardi's competitive spirit occurred away from football. He was an avid, though average, golfer—about a 12 handicap—who refused to accept strokes from anyone, no matter the difference in handicaps. He always played with better golfers, and often lost. But he kept trying to improve.

In 1965, Jack Nicklaus accepted an invitation to play an exhibition round at Oneida Golf and Riding Club in Green

Bay. Oneida was a lush and gorgeous layout of moderate difficulty. Lombardi used to shoot in the mid- to high 80's when he played there.

Nicklaus, Lombardi, Don Hutson, and the local pro, Bill Furnari, teed off in front of thousands of spectators. The pro, perhaps nervous because he was playing with the Masters champion, ballooned to an 83. Nicklaus shot a 74, respectable considering the fact that he had never seen the course and had attempted numerous crowd-pleasing shots. Lombardi scored a 79, his career best at Oneida.

Despite the apparent differences in our personalities, Vince Lombardi had a profound influence on me. My childhood years had prepared me for his style. Dad idolized MacArthur, quoted him frequently, and implemented his leadership style. He stressed the importance of reading about the great general and emulating him. Again and again he noted MacArthur's emphasis on the "will to win" when he discussed his wartime experience.

Lombardi's mentor at West Point, Red Blaik, was also devoted to MacArthur.

I quickly adopted Lombardi's organizational skills, preparation, and enthusiasm. I also maintained a distance between us.

My relationship with him was almost entirely on the professional level—I saw him socially only a few times, and even then it was by accident. When we did get together at a golf outing, our conversation invariably turned to football.

He left Green Bay to coach the Washington Redskins in 1969. Before he announced his decision he called me into his office.

"Bart, I'm leaving to coach the Redskins. I have mixed emotions about it, but it's a good move for me and my family."

"I'm going to miss you, Coach."

"I'm going to miss all of you and everyone in this city, Bart."

"Coach, I wish you the best of luck."

Lombardi thanked me and then paid me the highest compliment I'd ever received from him. He said, "I've observed the diligent way you've taken notes during our years together. Will you bring me your notes from all our game plans? They would really help me get started with the Redskins."

I brought him everything.

The following spring, after he had coached the Redskins for a season, Lombardi returned to Green Bay. Shortly after he arrived, he phoned and asked to come over to see our new home in De Pere, a small town just south of Green Bay. We proudly showed him around while he complimented Cherry on her contribution to the design and decoration of the house.

Finally we settled into the den. Cherry and I told him that most of what we had we owed to him. We never anticipated his reaction.

He bit his lip as his eyes moistened. Immediately we also began to choke up. Without saying another word, he quickly stood up and hugged and kissed Cherry. His only words were "Thank you," and he left.

That summer, I received word that he was dying of cancer. After a Saturday preseason game in Milwaukee, Zeke Bratkowski and I flew to Washington to see him. We were prepared to stay with him until Monday, when we had agreed to return to training camp, but he wanted no part of it.

We wanted to see him, but were nervous and didn't know what to expect.

He was emaciated and weak, no longer vibrant. He obviously didn't want anyone to see him in that condition, and after speaking with us a few minutes, asked his wife, Marie, to tell us he wished to be alone. Zeke and I left quietly, unable to talk until we reached the airport.

Coach Lombardi died on September 3, 1970, at the age of fifty-seven.

# CHAPTER

# 5

In 1959 Lombardi inherited a Packer team that had won only one game the previous season. If a team's record reflects the quality of its members, we should have expected a major housecleaning. The most dramatic change, however, occurred not in the area of personnel but in the degree of leadership provided by our head coach.

When Lombardi arrived, he quickly recognized that there were enough talented players on hand to form the nucleus of a winning football team. Initially, personnel changes occurred only in the areas in which he perceived that the team was most deficient. As a result, sixteen of the players in our 1959 starting lineup, eight on offense and eight on defense, were Packer veterans.

Our offensive line was comprised of Jim Ringo at center, Jerry Kramer and Fuzzy Thurston at guard, and Forrest Gregg and Bob Skoronski at tackle. Gregg and Skoronski were three-year veterans who were developing into dominating per-

formers. Kramer was a 1958 draft pick from the University
of Idaho. Thurston was acquired after having been released
by four different teams. Adding depth was Norm Masters,
who had been acquired in 1957 from the Lions as part of the
Tobin Rote trade. Masters could play either tackle and was
a dependable player who alternated with Skoronski.

Our wide receivers, Boyd Dowler and Max McGee, were
distinguished as much for their size as their speed. Dowler,
at six feet five, had sprinter's speed; McGee, at six-three, was
deceptively fast. Both were extremely difficult to bump off
stride. Boyd was the Packers' third pick in the 1959 draft
and became the NFL's rookie-of-the-year. At tight end, a
position that was becoming increasingly vital to the success
of a team's offense, Lombardi could choose from three talented athletes—Gary Knafelc, Ron Kramer, or Steve Meilinger. Knafelc and Meilinger had good speed for the position
while Kramer could run stride for stride with most wide
receivers.

At Lombardi's disposal were two future Hall of Fame
running backs, Paul Hornung and Jimmy Taylor. Paul was
the first player selected in the 1957 draft. Though he had
been a quarterback at Notre Dame, Lombardi planned to use
him as a multipurpose halfback in the same manner he uti-
lized Frank Gifford while coaching the Giants. Like Gifford,
Paul presented a significant threat to opposing defenses with
his ability to throw the option pass. Also like Gifford, he
was a slashing runner with a knack for picking up extra
yardage, especially near an opponent's goal line. Paul, however, at six-two and 215 pounds, was considerably bigger
than Gifford.

Taylor was a compact five-foot-eleven, 212-pound marvel
at fullback. His running style featured a nearly unstoppable
surge upon initial contact by defenders. Unlike most running
backs, he subscribed to the theory that the shortest distance
between two points was a straight line and enjoyed running
through defensive backs rather than around them. He was
used primarily as a blocking fullback at Louisiana State University, and was essentially an unknown when the Packers
drafted him in the second round in 1958.

Although the offensive lineup that would eventually produce two NFL titles for the Packers in 1961 and 1962 was
assembled before Lombardi arrived, many defensive changes
were to be made to our roster. The returning veterans in
1959, however, included a number of talented players on
defense. Included was a full compliment of linebackers in
Bill Forester, Dan Currie, Ray Nitschke, and Tom Bettis. We
played a 43 defense, which was the most prevalent at that
time. Forester, a Packer since 1953, and Dan Currie, our
number-one draft choice in 1958, played the outside positions. The middle linebacker position was shared by Bettis
and Nitschke, who became one of the greatest defensive players in pro football history.

Holdovers in the defensive backfield were John Symank,
Jesse Whittenton, Hank Gremminger, and all-pro safety Bobby
Dillon, who was at the end of his illustrious career. Lombardi
added outstanding safety Emlen Tunnell, who appeared to
be nearing retirement after eleven seasons with the Giants.
Tunnell, however, became a valuable leader and added three
years to his distinguished career.

Lombardi's biggest challenge in 1959 was to rebuild our
defensive line. Dave "Hawg" Hanner, the senior member of
the team and a fixture at defensive tackle since 1952, was
the only incumbent when Lombardi arrived. Unknowingly,
Cleveland's Paul Brown made Lombardi's task much easier.

First, Brown allowed Bill Quinlan to travel to Green Bay
in a trade involving Bill Howton and Lew Carpenter. Quinlan, a free-spirited individual who enjoyed himself off of the
field, spent four productive years in Green Bay. Henry Jordan
was also acquired from Cleveland in a trade that cost the
Packers only a fourth-round draft pick. Jordan was an undersize tackle by Cleveland's standards, but he possessed
great quickness. A year later, Willie Davis was acquired from
the Browns. Willie, like Henry, was considered too small for
Cleveland's defensive scheme. Willie became one of the most
dominating defensive ends ever to play the game and was
eventually inducted into the Pro Football Hall of Fame.

The defensive line was not the only area that Lombardi
set out to improve. Although I had completed my third NFL

season and felt that I was emerging as a mature quarterback, Lombardi lacked confidence in me as his leader on the field. This was evidenced by the trade he made with the St. Louis Cardinals for Lamar McHan shortly after he was hired by Green Bay. McHan had been the Cardinals' starting quarterback for most of the previous five years. St. Louis played in the same conference as the Giants, which meant Lombardi was very familiar with Mac's ability. McHan had good size, a strong arm, and was very competitive. He had been a single-wing tailback during his collegiate days at Arkansas and was a good runner when forced out of the pocket.

Concern over my future as a Green Bay Packer heightened during training camp, when McHan was quickly designated as the starter and I was left to compete against Babe Parilli for the backup spot. Matters became worse during our first scrimmage, when I threw an interception, which was followed by some not-too-constructive criticism from Lombardi: "One more like that and you're through!" It wasn't the last errant throw I made during training camp but I managed to survive. I had mixed feelings when Lombardi released Babe. Babe was four years older and I was retained primarily because of the difference in our ages. It was obviously not a vote of confidence from Lombardi. More difficult to accept, however, was the fact that I had displaced Parilli, my boyhood idol.

The Packers surprised the entire league when we defeated Chicago 9–6 in the opening game of the 1959 season. Pride in the Pack began to return to Green Bay, as we followed our victory over the Bears with two more at the expense of Detroit and San Francisco. I stood on the sidelines and watched the beginning of a great transformation.

In the fourth game of the season we hosted the Los Angeles Rams in Milwaukee, where the Packers continue to play some of their home games. The Rams brought us back to earth with a 45–6 embarrassment. The next week McHan injured his shoulder in our game against Baltimore and the Colts ran up thirty-eight points, defeating us easily.

Our next opponent was the New York Giants. The game

was of particular importance to Lombardi—it would be held in his hometown against a team he had coached for five years.

I worked extremely hard during practice the week prior to the game and had the game plan down cold. McHan didn't appear as though he would be able to play and I thought the game in New York would give me the chance to prove myself. Although Joe Francis and I divided practice time at quarterback that week, I was sure I would be called on if McHan couldn't answer the bell. Joe had been drafted in 1958 out of Oregon State University, where he played tailback in their single-wing offense. Now Lombardi was attempting to convert him to quarterback, and Joe was struggling at an unfamiliar position.

On Sunday, McHan started, but during our first offensive series it was obvious that his ailing shoulder prevented him from throwing the ball effectively. Lombardi was forced to take McHan out of the game, but I remained on the bench as Lombardi replaced McHan with Francis. The Giants defense ate him alive. While the Packers absorbed a 20–3 thrashing, I stood on the sidelines feeling unwanted and betrayed. I hadn't experienced so much frustration and helplessness since my senior year at Alabama. With me on the sideline was our talented tight end Ron Kramer, who was also held out of the game and was equally dejected.

Lombardi had already decided we would spend the night in New York. Ron and I showered quickly, returned briefly to our rooms, then set out to explore the bars of Manhattan and drown our frustrations.

I don't remember where we went that night or how many bars we went to. I don't know how much I drank or what I drank and I don't recall returning to the hotel. Fortunately, Ron was big and strong enough to carry me back. The only thing I do remember about that night is that it was the first and only time in my life that I have been drunk. With each succeeding drink, I became more convinced that Lombardi was responsible for my stupor. The next morning, I realized that sitting in a bar for four hours can cause as much discomfort as sitting on the bench.

McHan's shoulder had healed a week later when we faced the Bears in Chicago, but he sustained a leg injury in the final minutes of the first half. I replaced him for the remainder of the game. I had a disappointing performance, though, completing only three passes in ten attempts for 20 yards. The Bears beat us easily, 28–17.

McHan's second injury in three games and Francis's unconvincing appearance against the Giants led to my first starting role for Lombardi against the Colts in Milwaukee.

The game provided me with the long-awaited opportunity to prove myself as a starter to our new head coach. I knew that if I turned in an impressive performance, I might remain the starter for the rest of the season. On our first offensive series, however, I attempted to throw a pass that was batted into the air and landed in the arms of Big Daddy Lipscomb. I thought that Lombardi would pull me out of the game. Fortunately, I managed to prevent Lipscomb from returning the ball for a Colt touchdown when I knocked him out of bounds as he lumbered up the sideline. I hit Lipscomb so hard that I was dizzy for several seconds following the collision. As I returned to our bench, I braced for an explosion from Lombardi. His only comment, however, was, "Starr, I detest the damn interception but that was a fine tackle." Lombardi's astonishing reaction provided me with some assurance as I returned to the game and led the offense to a 462-yard day. Although we rallied from a 21–3 deficit at halftime, the performance failed to produce a victory, as we lost the game by a four-point margin, 28–24.

My performance in the game was less than outstanding, but I finally received a vote of confidence from Lombardi when, following the game, he told reporters, "Now I know I have two good quarterbacks."

The next week I was back in the starting lineup against the Washington Redskins, and led our team to a 21–0 victory. I connected on eleven of nineteen passing attempts, including touchdown strikes to McGee and Knafelc. Taylor and Hornung also had fine games, each rushing for 80 yards. But more important than any individual performance was our team's victory . . . we had snapped a five-game losing streak. Also, I felt we were beginning to perform as a cohesive unit. We controlled the ball with Lombardi's run-oriented offense and the defense responded with a shutout.

I remained the Packers' starting quarterback the rest of the season as we won four straight games, finishing with a record of 7–5. It was the Packers' best record in twelve years.

I was extremely encouraged by my performance in these last four games, completing fifty-two passes in seventy-nine attempts for 699 yards and six touchdowns. With each game during our brief winning streak, I gained more confidence in my ability to lead our team. In addition, I could detect that my teammates were beginning to believe in their quarterback for the first time since Tobin Rote was traded.

In the off-season of 1960, I studied composite films of John Unitas, Baltimore's established all-pro quarterback. Lombardi had compiled the films in order to isolate Unitas' throwing motion and ability to pump fake or look off defenders. We had similar deliveries, and Lombardi felt that by studying Unitas I could improve my passing ability. Unitas was a proven championship quarterback and I was not. I studied the films diligently. They provided a visual frame of reference from which I could improve the mechanics of my throwing technique, especially my follow-through. When I reported to training camp in July 1960, I felt that I was a more able and disciplined passer.

I was also coming off a strong finish from the '59 season and was thrilled to have earned the right to start at quarterback. Unfortunately, my happiness was short-lived. Chicago beat us at home by the score of 17–14, scoring all of their points in the fourth quarter.

McHan was a strong-willed individual who seldom hesitated to tell people what was on his mind. Lombardi was no exception. Following our opening loss to the Bears, Mac bluntly told Lombardi, "You should have been playing me." The next week against Detroit, he resumed the starting role. Lombardi must have liked his assertiveness.

I sat on the sidelines as McHan led the Packers to three

consecutive victories over Detroit, Baltimore, and San Francisco. Perhaps the most pivotal game in my career was our next one, at Pittsburgh. McHan started but struggled the entire first half, completing only four passes in sixteen attempts. He was frustrated because the offense was out of sync and upset because he felt our receivers were dropping passes that should have been caught.

Lombardi decided to start me in the second half. The Steeler defense was running a weak rotation zone in passing situations. When Knafelc ran a turn-in or hook pattern, the strong safety shot up to cover him, leaving Dowler in one-on-one coverage with a Steeler cornerback. Early in the second half, I connected with Knafelc on two short turn-ins. Later, with the Steeler secondary expecting another short pass to him, I sent Dowler down the middle on a deep post pattern. Dowler split the seam in the Steeler zone and was 5 yards from the nearest defender when he caught my pass to set up our only touchdown, a 1-yard plunge by Jimmy Taylor. Taylor's run and Hornung's four field goals in the first half were enough to beat the Steelers, 19–13.

Our victory did very little to ease McHan's frustration over being removed from the game. On the plane back to Green Bay, McHan said to Knafelc accusingly, "You never catch my passes the way you did today for Bart."

"That's because you never throw me the damn thing." Knafelc shot back. Mac continued to voice his displeasure, singling out Dowler, his friend and roommate, and said, "You didn't catch any of my passes." What could Boyd say?

When the plane landed in Green Bay, most of the players went to a local restaurant for dinner. Mac still hadn't settled down and marched right by a group of players to a separate dining room, where Lombardi was eating with some of the members of the Packers' executive committee. A couple of players tried to stop him but he was determined to voice his displeasure. He confronted Lombardi, and during the course of a heated conversation, called him a "Dago." Mac's days with the Packers were numbered.

Prior to our team meeting the next morning, Lombardi

called me into his office and said, "Your performance in the
Chicago game led me to believe that we had to make a change.
That's why I went with McHan. I haven't been all that happy
with his performances either, but stayed with him because
we were winning. After the way you brought us back yes-
terday, however, you're my quarterback and I'm not changing again." From that point forward, except when I was injured,
I started every game for the rest of my career.

Although I had secured the starting position, I don't think
Lombardi was totally convinced that I was the quarterback
he was looking for. Norb Hecker, a Packer assistant coach,
said that Lombardi saw leadership potential that could be
developed but questioned the strength of my arm. As a result,
he had an interest in obtaining a more established quarterback for at least another year.

Going into the sixth week of the 1960 season we had a
record of 4-1 and were in a tight race for the Western Conference title with the Detroit Lions, San Francisco 49ers, and
defending NFL champion Baltimore Colts. It was a new experience for all of us and, although we lost three of our next
five games, we still found ourselves in a three-way tie with
the Colts and 49ers with two games remaining. On Saturday,
December 10, our defense came up with a fantastic effort in
San Francisco to shut out the 49ers, 13–0. The next day in
Los Angeles the Rams upset Baltimore, and we were alone
in first place. A victory over Los Angeles in the final game
of the regular season would clinch a divisional title for the
Packers, their first since 1944.

The Packers stayed in a Santa Monica hotel that overlooked the Pacific. Gary Knafelc and I shared a room and
were so anxious that we could hardly sleep the night before
the game. We both were up before 5:30 A.M. and took a
relaxing walk on the sandy beach before meeting up with
the team.

During the pregame meal, a team official announced that
our bus departure for the Los Angeles Coliseum had been
moved up to 10:15 from 10:30. Gary and I, however, did not
hear the announcement, as we had left the dining room early

to get taped for the game. Consistent with our habit of adhering to "Lombardi Standard Time," we left our room at 10:15, thinking we would be at least ten minutes early for the team's departure. As we strolled through the hotel lobby, we saw a loaded bus with an angry head coach standing in its doorway. Lombardi spotted us and jumped off the bus. As he approached us, his finger was pointing, his face twisted in anger. While Gary and I checked our watches, Lombardi jumped our butts. I don't remember his exact words except that he said, "This will cost you a bundle." We figured it would be at least $50 each. It really shook me up, and all I could think about during the bus ride to the Coliseum was not allowing the incident to affect my performance. By the time the game started, it was the farthest thing from my mind.

We defeated the Rams 35–21 and won the Western Conference championship. After the game Lombardi stopped by, opened the door to the locker area that Gary and I shared in the visitors' dressing room and said, "Forget the fine."

That was it. He didn't compliment either of us by saying, "Nice game," or "Good going"; he just said, "Forget the fine." As he walked away from us, Gary snapped, "Thanks a lot, you old son of a bitch." Gary's spontaneous outburst put us both on the floor in laughter.

In Green Bay, the *Press-Gazette* put out a Sunday-evening special edition with a banner headline that read: PACKERS WHIP RAMS; ON TO PHILADELPHIA!"

The Eagles won the Eastern Conference with the best record in the NFL, 10-2. They featured Norm Van Brocklin, the talented quarterback who in his final pro season had thrown for 2,400 yards and twenty-four touchdowns, second only to Baltimore's John Unitas.

Successful coaches believe that championships are won primarily with a strong defense. The Eagles, however, were a team that possessed only a marginal defense. They were so lacking in talent that Chuck Bednarik, a thirty-five-year-old veteran of twelve seasons, played both center on offense and linebacker on defense. He played virtually the entire sixty minutes of the game, but Philadelphia's most dominating player was Van Brocklin. He was an inspirational leader and the closest thing I have ever seen to a one-man team.

Before the championship game, Jim Lee Howell of the New York Giants said, "I think the Packers are a better team than Philly, but they are a little weak at quarterback." Playing against Van Brocklin, I didn't need Howell's comments to motivate me.

We spent Christmas in Philadelphia, as the Eagles were hosting the championship game on December 26. At dinner the night before the game, Coach Lombardi presented each player with a tie in appreciation for having won the Western Conference title. Jim Ringo was hacked off over the fact that Lombardi couldn't think of something nicer than a tie to give us for such an important accomplishment. Following dinner, he gathered up about thirty ties and disappeared to his room with a few teammates. Later, when several players were returning from a walk, they looked up and saw Jim leaning out the window of his fifth-floor room, cutting the ties in pieces with a pair of scissors. It turned out to be one of the lighter moments of our trip.

The condition of Philadelphia's Franklin Field was atrocious. The ground had frozen during frigid weather in the weeks preceding the game. Then, unexpectedly, the weather warmed up and softened the ground on the field surface. Underneath, the ground was still icy, creating an inconsistency that affected everyone's performance. The footing was the worst I had ever encountered.

We jumped off to a 6–0 lead on a pair of Hornung field goals before the Eagles rallied to go ahead 10–6 at the half. Late in the third quarter, Philly was on our 4-yard line, but their scoring threat was stopped when John Symank intercepted a Van Brocklin pass in the end zone.

The Eagles held us to no gain on the next three plays before McGee faked a punt and scrambled 35 yards to a first down at the Eagle 46-yard line. Eight plays later we regained the lead at 13–10 when I connected with Max for a 7-yard touchdown and Hornung added the extra point. On the ensuing kickoff, Ted Dean had no problem with the mushy turf, returning the ball 58 yards to our 39. After a short drive, Dean scored from our 5-yard line to put the Eagles ahead, 17–13.

In the game's closing seconds, we began a six-play drive from our 35-yard line that reached the Eagles' 22. With fifteen seconds remaining, the clock running, and no timeouts, I threw to Jimmy Taylor in the flat. He ran through Eagle linebacker Maxie Baughan at the 15 and safety Don Burroughs bounced off of him at the 12. Bobby Jackson, a rookie defensive back who had just entered the game after the previous play, met Taylor at the 9-yard line. Taylor's legs were still churning, until Jackson was joined by Bednarik and several other Philadelphia defenders who collectively wrestled him to the ground. Time ran out and the Eagles won the NFL title, 17–13.

The game was a disappointing loss to say the least. It was especially hard for the veterans, who had endured the lean years in Green Bay only to come so close to winning it all. In the locker room, while heads hung in the wake of a heartbreaking defeat, Lombardi walked in and stood in the middle of the room with a defiant look. "The biggest tragedy of this loss," he said, "is that you guys didn't recognize that you were good enough to win." He was right.

Lombardi left us with one final thought. "We *will* win it all next year."

# CHAPTER

## 6

The 1961 season climaxed with one of the most lopsided victories in Packer history. I helped lead our team to the NFL championship, but earlier in the year I heard a rumor that made me wonder whether I would be playing at all.

Although we lost the 1960 championship game to the Eagles, I was confident in my ability to perform well in clutch situations. Coach Lombardi, however, apparently still had some doubts, and he expressed them at the 1961 league meetings that spring. Jim Kensil, the NFL's public relations director, had dinner one night with Lombardi and began to discuss the Packers' discouraging loss to Philadelphia. My name quickly became the center of discussion.

"Vince," he said, "let me ask you about Starr. I remember a play in which Max McGee was wide open for a long gain, but Starr didn't see him. What do you think?"

"Yeah, some guys see them and some guys don't," Lombardi answered curtly. "I'd really like to get Meredith. I'm willing to give the Cowboys any two players on our roster for him."

Don Meredith, an outstanding collegiate quarterback at Southern Methodist University, had just completed his first year with the Dallas Cowboys, who had just completed their first year in the NFL. Although Dallas failed to win a game, Meredith displayed flashes of the brilliant play that had led some pundits to label him "the best passer from Texas since Sammy Baugh." He was tall, mobile, strong.

Was Lombardi serious? Tex Schramm, the Cowboys' president, didn't think so. He knew that Lombardi coveted Meredith, but so did a number of other teams in the NFL. Tex never wound up offering Meredith to anyone, and Lombardi never pursued it. "I couldn't be sure whether Vince was sincere about a trade. He'd laugh and make flippant remarks, often intending to mask his true intent. We never reached meaningful discussions. I think Vince also knew that as an expansion team owner, there was no way I was going to trade our 'franchise' quarterback, particularly since he was a local hero."

Perhaps Lombardi was using this rumor as a psychological ploy to motivate me. If he was, he succeeded. When I heard that I might be playing second-string behind Meredith, I realized Lombardi still had doubts concerning my ability. My dad had also been skeptical, however, and I resolved back then to prove him wrong. I would react the same way now.

A few weeks later, Lombardi traded Lamar McHan, to Baltimore for a draft choice. Cherry and I knew then that I would be Lombardi's *only* field general.

After spending a few off-seasons in Birmingham, Alabama, Cherry and I decided to make Green Bay our permanent home. We moved out of the Ginsberg residence, bit the bullet, and purchased our first house, on Chateau Drive. We were delighted to be only a mile from Lambeau Field, but worried about the fact that we had taken on so much debt at 4 percent! In order to save money, I drove out to the country, dug up some birch and maple trees, hauled them back on a flatbed wagon, and planted them in our back-yard.

Our neighborhood was ideal for all three of us. We had moved in only a short time before Bart junior brought over a friend named Steve Crispigna. Later that day, I asked Bart and Steve if they would like to ride with me downtown to run some errands. As we walked up Walnut Street, I noticed a sign that said SAMMY'S PIZZA and asked the boys if they'd like one. Bart junior said, "Sure!" but Steve was somewhat shy. When we walked in, I was greeted by a man with curly dark hair and a genuine smile. "Hi. I'm Al Crispigna," he said. "I see my son is out hustling some business for me." Bart junior, Steve, and I sat down and enjoyed one beer, two Cokes, and the city's best pizza. When I discovered that the Crispignas lived directly across the street from us, I knew we had chosen the right community.

As our 1961 training camp began, optimism was high among the players, much higher than it had been just one year earlier. Our training camp was brutal, but we were now prepared for, and accustomed to, Lombardi's routines.

On opening day, we hosted the Detroit Lions in Milwau-kee. During the course of that afternoon, I managed to give the game away but gain additional confidence, thanks to Coach Lombardi.

The Lions were as well prepared as the Packers, and the flow of the game reflected how evenly matched we were. De-troit took a 14–10 lead into the locker room at halftime be-hind Nick Pietrosante's two touchdowns, but we hung tough and trailed only by 17–13 late in the fourth quarter. Using a no-huddle offense, we moved into position to score the winning touchdown, I glanced over at the down marker. It read 3. We needed about a foot for the first down, so I au-dibled a quarterback sneak. Unfortunately, it was actually fourth down, and I failed to gain the necessary yardage. The linesman forgot to flip the down marker to 4, but that didn't ease the embarrassment I felt after sneaking the ball and discovering I had turned it over to the Lions. When I walked to our sideline, however, Coach Lombardi saw how badly I felt and didn't say a word to me.

If ever there was a perfect occasion to berate me, that would have been it. But Lombardi's decision to let it pass signaled to me a new confidence, a new trust. When he first met me, he wondered whether I was perhaps so polite and modest that I wasn't tough enough to be a leader, to exert authority. He no longer had any doubts. During the next six weeks, we defeated our opponents by an average score of 35–6. We did play Minnesota, an expansion team, twice in that streak, but the other four teams were the 49ers, Bears, Browns, and Colts. We frustrated quarterbacks as talented as John Brodie, Bill Wade, Milt Plum, and Johnny Unitas. We ran over linemen as strong as Charlie Krueger, Doug Atkins, and Gino Marchetti. We destroyed teams coached by George Halas, Paul Brown, Weeb Ewbank. The game against Cleveland was particularly noteworthy.

The Browns were on a roll when we played them. After losing a close game to the Eagles in the first week, they defeated their next three opponents. They featured the NFL's greatest running back, Jim Brown. Most important, they would be hosting us in Cleveland Municipal Stadium, which held more than seventy-eight thousand spectators.

Lombardi decided we would conduct a special workout on Saturday in the cavernous arena. He gathered us together before practice and stressed the importance of not being intimidated by the crowd. The game also had a special personal meaning to him, because it was the first time he would coach against Paul Brown, the Browns' brilliant founder and leader. This was hardly the only intriguing matchup, however.

Jim Brown, their fullback, and Jim Taylor, ours, would be pitted against each other in a one-game battle that probably meant more to Taylor. Brown was the undisputed king of power backs, but Taylor intended to strip him of the crown. During our Saturday practice, Taylor spent every free minute encouraging our defensive players, almost pleading with them to play their best. They did. So did Jimmy.

Considering the quality of the opponent and the home-field advantage they enjoyed, our 49–17 thrashing was probably the best game we played all year. I had an outstanding day—fifteen for seventeen, 272 yards—but few noticed, because Jim Taylor had a career day. He ran over the Browns twenty-one times for 158 yards and 4 touchdowns. Jim Brown gained just 72.

We clinched the Western Conference title in the tenth game of the season with a 20–17 victory over the New York Giants. Our concentration was intense during the week leading up to the game, because we knew that the Giants, who were locked in a tight race with Philadelphia for the Eastern crown, might be our opponents in the championship game. We wanted to establish superiority and seemed ready to play as game day approached. We may have been too ready.

Our effort was supreme, but our execution was sloppy. I had one of the worst games of the year, throwing two interceptions and generally misfiring. Fortunately, Jesse Whittenton, our defensive right cornerback, came to the rescue and salvaged the game.

Early in the fourth quarter, the Giants led, 17–13, and had possession at their own 8-yard line. Our offensive players were exorting our defense to shut them down so we could get the ball back. Instead, Alex Webster, their bruising fullback, broke through our defensive line and headed upfield. As he crossed their 20-yard line, he ran into Henry Jordan and Jesse. Webster spun away from Henry, but his left arm flew up and Jesse reached in and stole the ball. Four plays later, Jim Taylor capped a 186-yard performance by smashing into the end zone from 3 yards out.

The fact that we won was no more important than the way we won—the Giants appeared to be dejected as they left the field following the game. Our attitude was one of relief, but also confidence. We knew that if the Giants couldn't beat us when we played this sloppily, they could never defeat us if we executed our game plan properly.

On December 31, 1961, Green Bay hosted its first championship game. We faced the Giants in a rematch that we knew would be no match. During the week, numerous stores displayed banners proclaiming Green Bay TITLETOWN USA. The residents were particularly proud of the local identification, since Milwaukee had been hosting some of the home games each year since 1935. In fact, Milwaukee has been the site for the last championship game the Packers hosted, in 1939. The Giants intended to make Green Bay "Tittletown," hoping that aging quarterback Y. A. Tittle would lead them to victory.

Perhaps the ultimate irony concerned the Packer coach. Wellington Mara, the Giants' owner, had wanted Lombardi to return to New York after Jim Lee Howell retired following the 1960 season. Lombardi, however, was contractually obligated to Green Bay and now was preparing to defeat Mara's team.

The 37–0 final score was not indicative of how thoroughly we dominated, how precisely we executed, how emotionally we played. We outgained New York 345–130. We had no turnovers. We wrapped up the game by halftime, leading 24–0.

The Giants keyed their defense on Jimmy Taylor. This was a wise decision, considering the results he obtained in our previous meeting, but we anticipated that they would be looking for him again. Jimmy was slightly hobbled by a leg injury, so I used him as a decoy. I threw three touchdowns and Paul Hornung rushed for 89 yards, winning the Most Valuable Player award. Paul's achievement was especially remarkable, since he had been on active duty in the army up until two days before the game.

None of the individual awards or team glory equaled the satisfaction I received after the game. Mom and Dad had been faithfully supporting me for years, and drove to Wisconsin every fall to attend a few games. Dad was less harsh than he used to be, patting me on the back, smiling. He never said much, however, and I knew he was thinking about Hilton, still comparing us. On this day, he finally let go.

When I opened the door to leave the building, Mom, Dad, and Cherry were waiting for me. Mom and Cherry rushed to embrace me, and, as I hugged them, I saw Dad looking at us with tears streaming down his face. He started to say something, stopped to gain his composure, then walked up and wrapped his arms around me. He gave me a big hug and softly whispered, "I was wrong, son."

# CHAPTER

## 7

The Green Bay Packers in the early 1960s were comprised of a diverse and fascinating group of individuals. Perhaps nowhere was the contrast between backgrounds and personalities better illustrated than in our starting offensive backfield.

Paul Hornung, our halfback, was capable of heroic feats on the football field. In our 45–7 rout of Baltimore in the fourth week of the 1961 season, he reached the pinnacle. He rushed for 111 yards on only eleven carries, ran for three touchdowns, caught a touchdown pass, kicked a 38-yard field goal and converted six extra points. The term "versatile" is generally overused, but not when describing Paul's unique skills.

His achievements on the playing field were no match for his nighttime conquests, however. His "golden boy" title was appropriate yet incomplete. One year, Paul traveled to the West Coast to play in the Pro Bowl. His roommate was Bill George, the Chicago Bears' middle linebacker. If Bill had any

thoughts of getting to know Paul, they were quickly dashed
when he discovered that Paul gets warmed up around the
time everyone else falls asleep. "My only roommate that
week was Paul's suitcase," Bill laughed.

Coach Lombardi's rule, prohibiting players from sitting
or standing at bars now carried a huge fine—$500. Paul,
however, knew something about getting his money's worth
and taking reasonable chances. One night before a game in
Chicago, he entered a posh North Side club, accompanied
by a gorgeous young blonde. Their table wasn't going to be
ready for thirty minutes, and she told Paul she would prefer
waiting at the bar, rather than the lounge. Chicago had
hundreds of restaurants, he figured, so why not? Paul and
his date pulled up to the bar and ordered a round. No sooner
had he taken his first sip than the blonde said, "That man
standing in the doorway is staring at you." Paul turned around
in disbelief. Lombardi smiled, walked up to him, and said,
"That'll cost you five hundred dollars. Have a nice evening."

We nicknamed him "Goat" because he had sloped shoulders, hidden by bulky shoulder pads. He was a large man—
six feet three, 215 pounds—for a halfback. Max McGee, the
only player who could keep the same hours as Paul, said,
"He has a forty-three-inch chest, and a thirty-six-inch head."

If anyone had the right to feel good about himself, it was
Paul. He was awarded the 1956 Heisman Trophy despite the
fact that Notre Dame won only two games that year. Green
Bay drafted him in 1957, and he quickly became one of the
league's most versatile performers—he was equally adept at
running, blocking, receiving, passing, and kicking. He led
the NFL in scoring three consecutive years, setting an all-
time league record of 176 points in 1960. Had he not suffered
a pinched nerve in his right shoulder during our 1960 championship game with the Eagles, we might have won the game.

Paul was a nonconformist, and a bachelor, so he and I
didn't socialize very often. However, our lockers were next
to each other for a number of years, and we became good
friends. He was as comfortable talking about social issues as
he was football. Most important, he was extremely thought-

ful and caring. Bart junior idolized Paul and begged me to
bring him into the locker room after practice so he could
talk to his hero. He must have come in hundreds of times,
but Paul always greeted him with a smile. Best of all for Bart
junior, Paul would inevitably ask Bart to bring him two
Cokes—one for the young fan, one for Paul. Bart was convinced that Paul hung the moon.

Our other back, Jim Taylor, may have been the toughest
football player I've seen. He was not particularly big (five-
eleven, 212 pounds), fast, or elusive, but he had a vicious
mean streak. He became angry every time he was tackled,
which meant he was always mad at two or three defenders
—one was never enough to stop him.

Jimmy was used to overcoming adversity. When he was
ten, his father died, so he began delivering newspapers at
4:00 A.M. to help support his family. While he was still in
high school, he worked in the Louisiana oil fields, swinging
a sledgehammer. This routine continued through his college
days at LSU. He also became such a devoted weight lifter
that George Allen commented, "He has the muscular structure of a two-hundred-and-thirty-pound man."

At LSU, Jimmy refined his blocking skills by leading the
way for sophomore sensation Billy Cannon. The Packers
drafted Jimmy in the second round of the 1958 draft. They
had a steal.

Jimmy's background and strength led to some incidents
that became legendary. Even Lombardi was shocked during
a game when Jimmy passed up an obviously clear path to
the end zone, changed direction, and blasted into a defensive
back. He still scored, but Lombardi asked him, "Why did
you run into him? You had a clear path to the end zone."

"You've got to sting 'em, Coach," answered Jimmy. "I
figure if I give the guy a little blast, he might not be so eager
to try and stop me next time."

When Jimmy decided he was going to do something, he
was going to do it. During training camp one year, he insisted
on driving the team bus from St. Norbert College, our training
headquarters, to our practice field. Fortunately for those of

us on board, the highway between the two locations is a straight line. We cruised down the road about fifty miles per hour, Jimmy at the controls, the players chatting about the upcoming season. Suddenly Jimmy walked right by us and sat down at the rear of the bus. About twenty players flew to the front to grab the wheel. One guy finally brought us to the field in one piece. We asked Jimmy what he was doing. "Just clowning around. We need to loosen the guys up a little," he said.

Jimmy saved his wildest antics for the playing field, however. He was especially crazy when we played eastern teams such as the Eagles or Giants. During one particularly rough game, Dick Modzelewski, the New York defensive tackle, came to the sideline and showed Sam Huff, their middle linebacker, an arm bloodied from wrist to elbow. "Sam, I'm telling you, Taylor bit me like a dog."

Sam said, "Dick, I warned you . . . that guy ain't human."

Despite the differences in background, style, and emotional makeup, Paul Hornung and Jimmy Taylor meshed into an ideal backfield. Their ability to work together was best illustrated by their success running the Packer sweep.

This play combined the raw power of the single wing with the finesse of the T formation. After taking the snap from the center, I faked as though I might hand off to Jimmy, who would dive straight ahead between right tackle Forrest Gregg and tight end Ron Kramer and block the opposing defensive end. The defense's respect for Forrest's and Ron's blocking and Jimmy's running opened the way for Paul. I completed my turn and handed off to Paul, who was moving to his right.

Paul followed guards Jerry Kramer and Fuzzy Thurston around the right side of the field, often for a large gain. Paul was adept at cutting back across the grain once the defenders began to close in. His uncanny knack of following blockers and picking his way through defenders was complemented by his strength, which he used to break tackles. The beauty of our sweep consisted of the ability of Paul and Jim to interchange roles. Each player took as much pride in his blocking as he did in his running.

Jimmy was the catalyst of Lombardi's "run to daylight" theory. In previous years, coaches designed plays that were precise, but also restricted a running back's natural instincts. If the play was designed to be run between the offensive tackle and the tight end, the running back was responsible for charging through that area whether a hole existed or not. Lombardi was one of the first coaches to modify this concept. If Taylor was running a slant play to the weak side, he had the option to run outside or inside, depending on the direction in which our left tackle, Bob Skorowski, blocked their right end.

Once again, the fact that Lombardi gave Jimmy an option was not as important as the reason for doing so. Lombardi recognized that defensive players over the years were becoming more skilled at reacting to blocks. As a result, it was increasingly difficult for an offensive lineman to block him in a certain direction. Lombardi took this defensive advantage and used it to our benefit. Our linemen were told to block the defender in whatever direction the defender allowed, and jimmy simply looked for the opening as he approached the line of scrimmage.

Coach Lombardi didn't have to design any special schemes for our middle linebacker, Ray Nitschke. About all that was required was finding a football field and some players wearing different jerseys; Ray took it from there. His background, however, hardly suggested a promising career in any profession.

Ray's father died when he was three, his mother when he was fourteen. Raised by his brothers in Maywood, Illinois, just outside of Chicago, he spent most of his time in the back room of a bar. Fortunately for Ray, he was such an outstanding athlete he was able to play his way out of the depressing conditions of his childhood. He was drafted by the St. Louis Browns as a baseball prospect, but chose to pursue football. His skills as a quarterback earned him all-state honors and a scholarship to Illinois. Ray's size and temperament led the coaches there to play him at both fullback and linebacker, where he excelled.

The Packers drafted him in the third round of the 1958

draft, but he didn't become a full-time starter until 1962. In his first few years he was not just tough and aggressive, he was unbridled and undisciplined. He also had to learn to control himself before the games.

In 1959, before a game against the Rams in Los Angeles, we also stayed in Santa Monica. Ray was just where he shouldn't be—in the hotel bar, drinking a beer—when Coach Lombardi and Phil Bengtson, the defensive coordinator, walked in the door. Most players would have turned away or slumped down. Not Ray. He yelled out across the room, "Hey, Coach! Phil! Come on over—I want to buy you guys a drink." Although Lombardi was no prude, he kept his distance from the players. He also knew how to deal with them. He simply stared at Ray until Ray sat back down. When he arrived at his hotel room, Lombardi called Bengtson and said he was going to send Ray back to Green Bay the next day. Phil talked him out of it and Ray nearly destroyed the Rams. Coach Lombardi couldn't help but smile as he watched his young middle linebacker hit every player who got near him.

Ray could take a hit as well as deliver one. During practice one day, as he was standing on the sideline, it began to rain. He decided to put his helmet on, and none too quickly. A gust of wind sent the team photographer's tower crashing down on Ray. A bolt protruding from the structure pierced Ray's helmet and stopped about a quarter of an inch from his skull. Ray crawled out from under the tower, cursing up a storm, unaware that his helmet had just saved his life.

Ray was one of the first true intimidators. "It's a matter of survival. If you don't like the contact, the violence, you might as well get off the field. My theory is simple: I will hit my opponent before he hits me and hit him harder than he hits me. That way, he'll always remember me." Ray's theory worked to perfection. On numerous plays, the opposing linemen were busy looking for him while he was busy making the tackle.

Ray never became completely disciplined on the field, however. During a game against the Redskins, Ray wandered about 10 yards away from his zone, picked off a pass, and lumbered upfield. As he ran toward our sideline, Coach Bengtson greeted Ray, saying, "Hell of an interception, Ray. You weren't supposed to be there, you know."

Ray replied, "No, I *was* supposed to be there. Here's the ball to prove it, right, Coach?" Bengtson turned to Lombardi and winked.

Off the field, with his premature baldness and horned-rim glasses, Ray looked like a CPA. On the gridiron, Ray had become the raging leader of Bengtson's defensive unit. Neither Bengtson nor Lombardi ever worried about their middle linebacker again.

Ray had the ability to humble all quarterbacks, including those on our team. Each year during training camp, the coaches held a long-throw contest. Only eight or ten players would participate, and at least one of the quarterbacks usually managed to heave one 65 or 70 yards. After everyone had completed his throws, Ray would step up, grab a ball, and fire it at least 20 yards beyond the second-best effort.

Ray's progress off the field may have been even more impressive. When he arrived in Green Bay, he was often too loud, too boisterous, too willing to party. But he gradually settled down, married, and became a model citizen.

Max McGee, on the other hand, has always remained the same. He arrived in Green Bay as a wide receiver from Tulane who was an incredible natural athlete. He was also one of the most astute players in the entire league.

During our 1960 championship game against the Eagles, Max was sent in to punt while we were trailing 10–6. Lombardi gave him specific instructions: "Don't gamble by running." When Max received the snap from center, however, he noticed that the Philadelphia punt-return players were quickly heading downfield. Max tucked the ball in his arm and nonchalantly followed them for about 30 or 40 yards. I was standing next to Lombardi and couldn't wait to see his reaction. He had to have mixed feelings—Max violated his order but his daring move led to a touchdown. As Max ran off the field, Lombardi patted him and said, "Way to go,

Max." Max said later that he wasn't taking an unreasonable risk—the field was wide open and he had to do it. Max's ability to read a defense, whether as a punter or as a receiver, helped Boyd Dowler quickly develop into another outstanding wideout. Max provided Boyd with more pertinent information concerning defenders in a month than Boyd learned in his high school and college careers combined.

Max also helped my development as a quarterback. He didn't say much, but when he did point something out, I was all ears. Max and Paul Hornung were fun-loving, free-spirited bachelors, and thus I seldom associated with them, except for an occasional beer. On the field, however, they were as serious as I, and often alerted me to changes in the defensive coverage so I wouldn't have to waste a play while discovering them myself.

After playing well as a rookie in 1954, Max was called into active duty in the air force for two years. It didn't take long for his superiors to find out he was an innovative player in any sport.

While stationed at flying school in Laredo, Texas, Max took off on a solo flight, became disoriented, and ran out of fuel. He finally landed on a duster strip among the fruit orchards of Magic Valley, near the Rio Grande. Max never panicked, borrowing some fuel and a highway map from the duster pilot. He didn't know if he had the right octane for his T-6, but he did have an accurate map. He finally arrived about two hours late, with the control tower desperately trying to find him. Max came roaring in without ever acknowledging radio contact until he was on his final approach.

The next day, he found himself in front of the air force board of review, charged with breaking at least twelve regulations. He might have been punished, except for the fact that his instructor pleaded for leniency. He knew that Max had the kind of initiative required to be a great pilot. Max remained in the program.

After graduating, Max tried his hand at teaching young pilots. Air force tradition required student pilots to give their instructors a fifth of whiskey after completing a solo flight.

One of Max's students was struggling, but Max urged the kid to try his solo flight. On Max's last day on base before being transferred to Eglin, the student soloed his way into a tree.

Max rushed over and asked him, "Are you OK?"

The kid answered, "I think I'll be all right."

"Good," said Max. "You owe me a fifth of whiskey.

One of the few players who could match Max's all-around skills was Jesse Whittenton, one of our talented defensive backs. Like Max, he was a free spirit who was able to adapt to, and excel within, the Lombardi system. He was a tough Texan with a cowboy look and swagger. After starring as a quarterback at Texas Western, he was drafted by the Rams and then traded two seasons later to the Bears. Jesse developed a severe stomach virus that threatened to ruin his season. George Halas, the Chicago coach, gave him the option of going on injured reserve or trying out with another team. Jesse chose the Packers over the Lions and stepped right into a starting role. In 1961, he was a unanimous all-pro. Three years later, however, at age thirty, he walked away from football.

Jesse was as proficient at striking a golf ball as he was at covering a wide receiver. A friend of his from El Paso offered Jesse the opportunity to purchase a golf course with no down payment. Jesse checked it out and discovered that it was rattlesnake-infested but had potential. More important, he discovered a young golfer he wanted to sponsor. Jesse told Lombardi about this opportunity and Lombardi gave him his blessing.

"By the way, Jesse, what's the name of this kid you're so excited about?" asked Lombardi.

Jesse said, "Coach, you'll be hearing about him soon. His name is Lee Trevino."

The greatest pure athlete on our team was neither Max nor Jesse, however. Ron Kramer, our right end, was the most impressive physical talent I have ever seen. He was also the most enigmatic.

Ron was six feet three and 245 or 250 pounds, depending on the time of year. Unlike most players, he often gained weight during the season. He was incredibly strong, yet agile enough to be an all-Big-10 basketball player at Michigan. He was bright and articulate, but often pensive and quiet.

The three qualities Ron possessed that never varied were his running, catching, and blocking abilities. He was consistently one of the fastest players on our team, despite his size. Had he taken football a little more seriously, he might have gone down as the greatest tight end in history.

There is a common theme in the most inspiring stories regarding the 1961 Packers. Willie Davis, Herb Adderley, Elijah Pitts, and Willie Wood all rose from disadvantaged backgrounds to make major contributions to the success of the Green Bay Packers.

When Vince Lombardi signed Willie Wood as a free agent in 1960, the Packers had only two or three returning black players. That hardly deterred Willie, however, as he was used to overcoming tall odds. During pickup basketball games growing up in Washington, D.C., Willie played toe to toe with Elgin Baylor. Willie held his own.

Willie accepted a scholarship to the University of Southern California, and he blossomed as a quarterback. He was only five-ten, but USC employed an offensive scheme that gave him the option to run or throw. In the second game of his senior year, he fractured his left collarbone. Still, he was confident he would be drafted the next year by some National Football League team. He never received a call.

The teams had several excuses for not drafting Willie. He was too injury-prone. He was too short. He didn't throw the ball often enough. The fact of the matter, however, is that none of those excuses would have prevented a team from drafting him had he been white.

Undeterred, Willie called the Packers during one of our trips to Los Angeles. He asked for a tryout, nothing more. Lombardi gave him one and signed him the following year.

It took Willie about ten minutes during our first practice to make the Packers realize they had somebody special. He outhustled everyone on special teams, covered receivers like a blanket, and returned punts better than anyone in the league.

In his second year, 1961, he replaced the venerable Em Tunnell as the starting right safety. During the next twelve years, he may have missed a total of two or three tackles. I hope his consistently brilliant play will someday lead him to the Hall of Fame.

Willie Wood's running mate in the defensive backfield, Herb Adderley, has already been enshrined. He may have been the best defensive back to play the game, but his greatest accomplishment was just staying alive.

Herb grew up in the heart of Philadelphia's ghetto, where a kid either rises or falls. Herb's closest brother fell and fell hard. He became involved with drugs and crime, and eventually was convicted of first-degree murder. Herb knew it could just as easily have been him. He realized that he had to get out, and he did. He was a high school star in football and track. When he enrolled at Michigan State, he became an all-Big-10 halfback and world-class hurdler. He improved at every level of competition, and his professional career continued that trend. Ironically, however, his diverse skills almost cost him the chance to become a superstar.

Lombardi chose Herb in the first round of the 1961 draft with the intention of keeping him on the offensive line of scrimmage. He knew that he could provide some added speed to the backfield, but Herb knew that Jim Taylor and Paul Hornung would still be starting. Lombardi discussed the possibility of playing wide receiver behind Boyd Dowler and Max McGee. Herb told Lombardi he wanted the opportunity to start. Lombardi was delighted that his prize rookie wanted to play so badly, and installed him in the left cornerback position. Herb became a starter during his rookie year and an all-pro the next.

"It scares me to think I almost put him in the wrong position," Lombardi said. "Good running backs are a dime a dozen; great defensive backs are rare. They must possess a unique combination of speed, daring, and mental toughness."

Herb lacked nothing. He was polite off the field but ornery on it. He intimidated receivers with his size—six-one, 210

—and strength. Best of all, he was the quintessential big-play man.

During a game against the Vikings in Minnesota, Herb not only blocked a potential game-winning field goal, he completely smothered it. The snap and kick were perfect, but Herb simply would not be denied as he sprinted around the left side of the Viking line and dove for the ball. Hank Gremminger, an excellent cornerback whose ability was too often overlooked, picked up the ball and sprinted 80 yards for a touchdown, but Herb was the player we saluted after the game.

Herb's ability to read the quarterback's eyes and receivers' moves resulted in numerous touchdown returns over the years, but it also restricted his opportunities. After a few years, opponents just quit challenging him.

Willie Davis was as outstanding a defensive end as Adderley was a defensive back. And, like Adderley and Wood, he was an inspiring, classy individual.

He claimed to receive his nickname, "Dr. Feelgood," from the girls when he was growing up because "I made them feel good." No doubt about it—he made everyone feel good. He reported to practice with his great smile and enthusiasm every day. He said on many occasions how lucky he was to be well paid for playing the game he loved.

Willie grew up without much guidance from his father, who was seldom around. But his mother, Nodie Davis, a kitchen worker at a Texarkana, Arkansas, country club, helped Willie develop his positive attitude. She insisted that Willie and her two other children get an education. They all did.

Willie graduated from Grambling and was a seventeenth round draft choice of the Cleveland Browns in 1956. After spending two years in the army, Willie returned and was bounced back and forth between the offensive and defensive lines. In 1959 he played backup offensive tackle. The following year the Packers traded for him. But he was planning to play in Canada. "In my first few years, the Cleveland coaches used to threaten us. They'd say, 'If you don't produce, we'll send you to Green Bay.' I wanted no part of it."

Coach Lombardi heard about Willie's plans and called him. "Willie," he said, "I want you to know that *I* initiated the trade. I remember playing against you when I was coaching at New York. You always gave a hundred percent. I want you on my team."

Willie reported and was rewarded with a $1,000 bonus on his contract. He started every game—preseason, regular season, postseason—during the next ten years.

He didn't possess the size—six-three, 240—the Browns wanted, but he had the quickness, tenacity, and intelligence Lombardi looked for. His desire to excel led to an MBA from the University of Chicago and a successful business career based in Los Angeles.

Despite the fact that Green Bay had practically no black residents, Willie Davis was a gregarious man and positive enough to find a way to fit in and have a good time wherever he was. He was also extremely caring. When he heard that Lombardi was dying of cancer, he immediately boarded a plane in San Diego and flew all night to see his coach. Davis tried to cheer him up, but Lombardi simply said, "Willie, you're a fine man. I appreciate everything you did for me." They were both in tears as Lombardi said, "Good-bye, Willie. Pray for me."

While Willie Wood, Herb Adderley, and Willie Davis immediately stepped into starting positions with the Packers, it took Elijah Pitts a few years before he found the limelight. He was Green Bay's thirteenth-round draft choice in 1961 from Philander Smith, and he arrived as a bashful, insecure young running back. Paul Hornung was our star and Elijah was now competing against him for the starting halfback position. Elijah must have been pleasantly surprised, then, when Paul decided to take him out on the town. Paul made him feel a part of the team, a part of the community. It was just as Lombardi had preached to us.

Vince Lombardi has been honored for everything except the quality that was probably more important than any other—his continual emphasis on the need for us to help each other. And he did everything he could to relieve the social isolation that the black players had to endure, both at home and on the road.

Bob Skoronski, our offensive tackle, recalls one of Lombardi's most inspiring speeches. He noted that Lombardi said, "It's easy to love something beautiful, something bright, someone glamorous. However, it takes a special person to love something unattractive, someone unknown." Lombardi explained that some of the players on the team were going to be famous, some obscure, but everyone was equally important. For us to succeed, we had to place our personal goals behind those of the team. We had to pick each other up and push each other to higher levels. Paul didn't have to help Elijah, but Paul was more concerned with helping Elijah than helping himself. This type of love for each other probably best explains the fact that we won five NFL championships in seven years.

# CHAPTER

## 8

One of the most dominant teams in the history of professional football came very close to not even playing in a championship game. In 1962, there were no wild-card games, no home-field advantage based on record. Our team began the season knowing we had to win the Western Conference to earn the right to play the Eastern Conference champions for the title. We also realized that the title game, if we made it that far, would be held at the Eastern Conference's home field, no matter what the records of the opposing teams. Our biggest concern, therefore, was Detroit. The Lions had a talented and hungry team, having finished second to us in our conference in 1961.

After destroying our first nine opponents—six preseason, three regular season—we hosted the Lions in game four. Detroit was also undefeated, and the crowd was buzzing as the fans entered Lambeau Field on a cool autumn afternoon.

We came close to giving the game away, then took it away.

Statistically, we outgained the Lions all day. We outrushed them. We outpassed them. Unfortunately, we also turned the ball over four times, and Detroit led, 7–6, late in the fourth quarter.

With less than a minute to play, the Lions had possession of the ball near midfield. It was third down, and, as they approached the line of scrimmage, I asked Paul Hornung, "Do you think we'll get another shot?"

Paul said, "I hope so. I'm ready." Paul was handling the field-goal kicking and wanted desperately to win the game with a last-minute kick.

But Paul and I feared that the Lions would simply run Nick Pietrosante, their powerful fullback, up the middle. If he gained the yardage necessary for a first down, the game would be over. Even if he didn't, the Lions would send in safety Yale Lary, the NFL's most effective punter, to kick the ball, forcing us to sustain a lengthy drive to win. The Lions' defense had been playing us tough all day, capitalizing on our miscues and holding us to two field goals. Most of our players were standing, but the mood was one of disappointment and frustration, not excitement.

Milt Plum, the Lions' quarterback, walked up to the line of scrimmage, barked the signals, and . . . dropped back to pass. I couldn't believe it. Surely he was going to run a quarterback draw, not throw the ball downfield. I was wrong. Not only did he throw it downfield, but he threw it toward Terry Barr, who was being covered by Herb Adderley, our best athlete. Barr slipped slightly, but Herb planted his feet cleanly, stepped up, and intercepted the pass near our 45-yard line. I almost ran onto the field right then, I was so excited. Herb wove through the Lion offensive players until he was finally tackled inside their 20-yard line. We mobbed him as the crowd burst into delirium. Their emotional level was nothing compared to that of Alex Karras, however.

After conferring with Lombardi and agreeing we should run the ball toward the middle of the field to get good field-goal position, I ran to our huddle to call our first play. I heard Karras, their volatile defensive tackle, swearing at the top of his lungs at Plum for throwing the ball: "You stupid son of a bitch, what the hell were you doing . . . ?" Alex halted his tirade, put on his helmet, and joined his teammates in their defensive huddle. We ran the ball to the 14-yard line, brought in our field-goal unit, and listened to Alex's continuing outburst. I did not envy Jerry Kramer, our right guard, who had been lining up across from Alex all day.

We had only to convert the field goal to win the game. Jim Ringo's snap was perfect. I placed the ball on the turf, spun the laces toward the goalposts, and watched Paul's foot whizz just under my hand. The ball sailed through the goalposts and into the stands.

The game was decided by a defensive player, Herb Adderley, which was appropriate that day. But Alex Karras remained convinced that an offensive player, Milt Plum, was responsible, and Karras' diatribe could be heard by players, officials, and fans as we exited the field.

In 1962, both teams exited Lambeau Field through the same tunnel, at the north end of the stadium. To make matters worse, or at least more uncomfortable, the opponents' locker room was separated from ours by nothing more than a ten-foot hallway. The doors on each end of the hallway were usually enough to prevent us from hearing the commotion next door, but not on that day.

For the first time since Lombardi joined the Packers, his postgame comments were interrupted. It was Alex again. In the visitors' locker room, he tore off his helmet, threw it at Plum, and hit him squarely in the chest. Lions head coach George Wilson jumped between them to prevent pandemonium from breaking out, and said: "Look, guys, it's my fault. I made the call."

As a matter of fact, Plum made the call, but Wilson tried to take the heat off him and get the players' minds off the game. "Hey, guys, shower up and let's get out of here."

Wilson's thinking was sound, but the showers refused to cooperate.

When the Detroit players filed into their shower facilities, they received another slap in the face when nothing more

than cold water trickled out. A few minutes later, the Lions'
equipment manager knocked on our door. "Dad" Braiser,
our equipment manager, greeted him.

"What do you want?"

"I need to see Vince Lombardi."

"What for?"

"Our showers aren't working: We can't get much water
and what does come out is ice cold."

"Dad" told Lombardi about the problem and he decided
to let the Lions use our showers. I was glad I had already
finished, as I didn't need any more tension that day. For the
next twenty or thirty minutes, our shower facility was silent
except for the water streams from the shower heads.

When the Lions dried off and walked back to their locker
room, I expected them to be discouraged. They were outraged. As their last player exited, he headed toward the hallway, stopped, and said, "See you in Detroit."

Did they ever.

The Lions had been hosting the Packers every Thanksgiving since 1952. With each succeeding year, the event grew
in popularity and intensity. By 1962 it had become a national
tradition for sports fans to turn on the tube and watch football
on Thanksgiving. Vince Lombardi, however, detested the
game.

Lombardi was the most organized and disciplined coach
I've ever seen. He loathed anything that would throw us off
schedule, or disrupt our routine.

In order to play on Thanksgiving Day, we had to fly to
Detroit on Wednesday afternoon. And since we had to recuperate from Sunday's game by taking it easy on Monday,
we had only this one day of intense practice before we had
to play. So our concentration wasn't what it should have
been on the day before the game.

That would normally be enough to cause trouble by itself,
but in 1962, it was compounded by the Lions' anger and
desire for revenge.

By the time the first half had ended, Detroit led 23–0. It
seemed much worse. I was sacked six or seven times, in-

cluding once for a safety by Roger Brown, their six-foot-six, 300-pound defensive tackle. Lombardi didn't have to say much in the locker room. We had played listlessly, while the Lions performed as though they intended to give us a cold shower in front of the entire nation.

The Lions continued to pour it on and were winning 26–0 at the end of the third quarter. The rout was on and the Detroit fans loved it.

Although the Lions were clearly the superior team that day, the character of our team surfaced in the fourth quarter, when we outscored Detroit 14–0, despite the fact that their defensive line was teeing off on every play. As we walked off the field, I *knew* we would destroy our next opponent.

We defeated Los Angeles the following week, 41–10.

With two games left in the 1962 regular season, our record was 11-1; the Lions were 10-2. We knew that we would be the Western Conference champions if we won our remaining two games against San Francisco and Los Angeles. For the second time in three years, our West Coast trip would determine whether we'd be making one to the East Coast.

San Francisco intended to limit our trips to one. They took a 21–10 lead at the half behind the brilliant play of quarterback John Brodie and receiver Bernie Casey. To make matters worse, the Lions were playing the Vikings that weekend. The Minnesota franchise was only two years old and we knew they would be no contest for Detroit.

Lombardi sensed our frustration. He occasionally yelled at us at halftime, but never in a panic-stricken manner. Today he didn't even have to raise his voice. He was at his peak when under pressure. The myth of Lombardi states that he was explosive at halftime and on the sideline, overemotional, almost out of control. The fact of the matter is that he was all business. His outbursts were serious but never overblown. He was a master at analyzing an opponent and implementing adjustments.

The 49ers game would have been the perfect opportunity for him to lose his cool, but he remained quite calm. He said, "Men, there is nothing wrong with our game plan, nothing

lacking in your effort. The only thing missing is your concentration and execution. Don't worry about the Lions or the
standings. Just bear down. Everything else will fall into place."
We scored on our first two possessions in the third quarter
and defeated the 49ers, 31–21.

Lombardi's postgame speech was short and sweet.

"Men, that second half was Packer football. Nice going."

The mood in our locker room was a combination of relief
and satisfaction. We could relax, after all, since the Rams
were next up on the schedule. Los Angeles had won only
one game all season and we had killed them earlier that year.

Someone forgot to remind the Rams that they were supposed to lie down when we played them. Two rising young
stars, quarterback Roman Gabriel and defensive tackle Merlin Olsen, led a charged-up Los Angeles team that nearly
knocked us off before succumbing, 20–17. We were lucky
to be playing the Giants again for the title. We were unlucky
in having to play them in New York.

For many years, the National Football League determined
the home team in the championship game by alternating
conferences annually. In 1959 the Baltimore Colts hosted the
New York Giants, despite the fact that the Giants had a better
regular-season record. Why? Because in 1959 it was the
Western Conference champions' turn to do so. In 1962 that
advantage fell to the Eastern Conference champion.

The weather on game day, however, was imported from
Green Bay. It was 15 degrees and blustery. When we woke
up for our pregame meal, I remember being approached by
a Giants' fan in our hotel. He said, "I'll bet you're delighted
with the weather. Boy, what an advantage for you guys."

He would have lost his bet.

I didn't like playing in weather like that any more than
anyone else. I grew up in Alabama, not Alaska. Besides, as
quarterback, I preferred warm weather because it allowed
me to grip the ball better and throw it with an easy, relaxed
motion. Physically, therefore, I don't believe we had an advantage over the Giants.

Psychologically, we had them right where we wanted

them. The Giants *thought* we liked to play in weather like
that. We never actually enjoyed such adverse conditions, but
we were more accustomed to it, and if the Giants wanted to
think we liked it, fine. If they had been able to take a close
look at our game plan, however, they would have never given
it another thought.

Our strategy called for an emphasis on passing. We were
extremely confident that our line could handle their pass
rush and that our receivers could beat their defensive backs.
Unfortunately, our plan flew out the window when we walked
onto the field for our warm-ups. The Bronx winds were
whipping us at fifty miles per hour, blowing debris into the
air and pregame passes back in my face. When I saw our
team benches continually being tipped over by the wind, I
knew we had to make a major adjustment. I told Coach Lombardi that we would have to be very selective in the types
of passes we chose to throw.

"Coach, I'm going to have to be a little more conservative."

"I know, Bart. As long as we can keep them off balance . . ."

Willie Wood was unable to kick off the first three times
he tried to do so, because the wind quickly knocked the ball
off the tee. Finally, one of our coverage men held the ball
and the game began.

If Y. A. Tittle, the Giants' quarterback who threw thirty-
three touchdown passes during the regular season, thought
he might add to that total during this game, he was in for a
rude awakening. During the Giants' first series, he threw a
quick out to his favorite receiver, Del Shofner. Just about the
time he released the ball, the wind gusted and knocked the
ball down about 3 yards in front of his intended target. Tittle
and Shofner looked at the ball, shrugged, and trotted off the
field as the New York punting unit came on. If Y. A. Tittle
had this much difficulty with the wind, I saw no need to
fight it.

However, as hard as I tried to ignore the conditions and
concentrate on our task, it was nearly impossible. I remember

one particular sequence when the wind finally died down as we approached the line of scrimmage. The Giants' defense was crowding the line, but I had already called a running play. It was the perfect time to call an audible and attempt a long pass.

Incredibly, as if on cue, the New York crowd turned up its decibel level, and I knew that our receivers couldn't possibly pick up an audible. This game would be decided on the ground and by turnovers.

Our defensive unit shut out New York for sixty minutes. This was becoming commonplace, as they had already done so three times during the regular season. Four other times, they held our opponents to seven points or less.

Offensively, we controlled the Giants with conservative running plays and an occasional pass. Jim Taylor gained 85 hard-fought yards in his head-to-head duel with Sam Huff, New York's outstanding middle linebacker and defensive leader.

Lombardi and I conferred more during this game than any other I can recall. After we recovered a fumble on the New York 28-yard line, I looked at him, smiled, and said, "How about it, Coach?"

He replied, "Have at it."

I entered the huddle and called for Paul Hornung to throw an option pass. It was the first time all day we had tried a truly daring move, and I could sense our excitement.

I took the snap from Jim Ringo and handed off to Paul, who swept right. Our guards pulled in front of him to meet the Giant defenders, who were sprinting toward Paul. Most of them took themselves right out of the play as Paul slowed up and lobbed an easy toss to Boyd Dowler for a 21-yard gain. We had executed perfectly a play designed to capitalize on the letdown a team often experiences after a turnover.

What would be the reaction of the Giant defense now that they were backed up to their 7-yard line? I decided that they would be extremely aggressive but still somewhat unsure of themselves. As a result, I called for Taylor to run a slant play behind a cross-blocking scheme. One of our linemen was able to get a piece of Huff, and Jimmy slipped through a narrow crack to the end zone.

The only major error we committed that day occurred in the third quarter, when the Giants blocked a punt and returned it for a touchdown. Otherwise, our special teams played as well as our offense and defense. Jerry Kramer, who became our field goal kicker in midseason after Paul Hornung injured his knee, connected from 26, 29, and 30 yards on the slick field.

After the game, some New York sportswriters suggested that the results might have been different had the game been played in better conditions. I agree. We would have beaten them by more than nine points.

More rational reporters across the country wondered whether the 1962 Packers were the greatest team in history. It is as valid a question today as it was then. How can we compare teams from different eras? Obviously, we can't. All we can do is determine how well a given team stacked up against opposing teams. Here, then, are the facts:

Both defensive ends, Willie Davis (first team) and Bill Quinlan (second team) were consensus all-pros. Willie was probably the most dominating defensive end in the NFL that year.

Defensive tackle Henry Jordan was also a first team all-pro performer. He enjoyed one of his finest seasons. His opponents did not. Our other tackles, Dave Hanner and Ron Kostelnik, received less recognition because they were the designated "spy" tackles, responsible for staying home while Henry gambled recklessly in pursuit or pass rush.

When all-pro first-team linebackers were announced, we came very close to sweeping the awards. Bill Forester and Dan Currie were first-team selections; Ray Nitschke settled for second team only because Joe Schmidt had a remarkable season at middle linebacker for the Lions.

Our defensive backs didn't take a backseat to anyone, either. Left cornerback Herb Adderley and safety Willie Wood were first-team selections; Jesse Whittenton made the second team as a cornerback, and Hank Gremminger had a terrific year, intercepting five passes.

The only position in which we didn't place any all-pros was wide receiver, but Max McGee and Boyd Dowler caught forty-nine passes each and would have had many more had we not run the ball so effectively.

Ron Kramer, our tight end, was a first-team all-pro for his devastating season. So was Forrest Gregg, our right tackle, for the same reason. Guards Jerry Kramer and Fuzzy Thurston made first and second team, respectively. Jim Ringo was his usual self and first-team awards followed. Bob Skoronski, our left tackle, was typically and unjustly overlooked.

I led the league in passing efficiency on my way to a first-team selection. When I wasn't throwing the ball, I handed off to Jim Taylor, who led the league in rushing and scoring. He was the league's Most Valuable Player.

Out of twenty-two all-pro positions, we captured eleven first-team awards and four second-team honors.

As a team, we scored the most points, thirty per game, allowed the fewest, ten per contest, and lost only one game out of twenty-one, all games included.

It's difficult to prove that one team is the best of all time, but the 1962 Green Bay Packers have to be considered one of the most dominant in the modern years. Eight players—Ringo, Gregg, Taylor, Hornung, Davis, Nitschke, Adderley, and I have been inducted into the Hall of Fame, along with Lombardi.

Jimmy Taylor's incredible season led to an improved passing attack, since our opponents became preoccupied with stopping him. As I improved my quarterbacking skills, we in turn developed a sound, well-conceived strategy that made our running game even more effective. Lombardi stressed ball control, whether it be on the ground or through the air. However, 1962 was also the first year in which I became known as a bold field general, particularly in short-yardage situations.

After one of our games, a 49–0 victory over the Eagles in

Philadelphia, Cherry and I were walking downtown and were approached by a Packer fan.

"Hey, Bart, you guys played great Sunday."

"Thanks very much. We were hot."

"Bart, I want to tell you, I love the way you gamble on third or fourth and short. It seems like you complete a long pass every time in that situation."

We concluded our chat and he wished us good luck. He obviously had no way of knowing our strategy and thus was simply inaccurate in describing those calls as gambles. In fact, the calls were high-percentage plays.

When an opposing team was attempting to stop our attack, their first concern, of course, was the running of Taylor. Their determination to slow or stop him became even greater once he had already picked up some yardage against them. As a defensive player, the greatest incentive to nail him occurred during short-yardage situations, since stopping him meant they would receive possession of the ball.

As I approached the line of scrimmage under that scenario, I could see the defensive line bunched up together in a short-yardage defense. There is no way a defensive lineman can rush the quarterback once he's on all fours with his nose six inches above the ground.

The linebackers usually crept closer to the line of scrimmage. Who could blame them? They didn't want Jimmy to get up a head of steam, and we were obviously going to run him right at them. The Packers in general, and Lombardi in particular, liked to run the safe, high-percentage play, as scouting reports indicated. After all, one of the reasons the Packers were so successful was that we controlled the ball.

Most defensive backs were guilty of reacting too quickly to a run fake. If Taylor came roaring through the line, they had to be prepared to meet him head on, lest he run all the way into the end zone. Our receivers were glancing toward the middle of the field, where Jimmy was to carry the football.

As I took my position under center, I could see that the

defense was pumped up to stop Jimmy. We were determined to have him gain the necessary yardage.

I received the snap from Ringo, turned, and handed off to Jimmy, who smashed into the line, without the ball. The odds were now in our favor.

Boyd Dowler, Max McGee, and Ron Kramer were tough enough for defensive backs to cover under normal circumstances. When the defensive backs were all alone, with no help from their linebackers and weak-side safety who were thinking run, the result was a mismatch.

My first objective was to find one of our receivers deep downfield. They were smart and sure-handed, so I simply had to throw the ball away from the defensive back; they would adjust to the ball and make the catch. In the unlikely event they were covered, I dumped the ball off to an alternate receiver who had run a shorter route.

How often were we successful? Nearly every time. I can recall only one occasion in which the short-yardage "play action" pass did not work, but it happened on a third down, meaning we simply had to punt.

Why did it work? First, defenses didn't adequately stress the need to prevent the big play. Second, we had a strong running game. Third, the great simulated run blocking by our offensive line. Finally, we used the element of surprise. I didn't call the play *too* often. During a game against Cleveland, I decided to put it to the ultimate test.

The Browns had driven to our 1-yard line but failed to score on fourth down. As our offense ran onto the field, I was convinced that the Cleveland defenders would crowd the line of scrimmage and try to stuff us. Knowing they would probably be looking for Taylor, I decided it would be a perfect opportunity for a surprise pass.

Tom Moore, our halfback, approached the Cleveland outside linebacker as if to throw a block for Jimmy. Just as their linebacker planted his feet in anticipation of a hard block, Tom dipped outside and began to sprint up the left sideline. The linebacker turned to catch up, but Tom was already 5 yards beyond him. I hit Tom in full stride and he ran untouched into the end zone for a 99-yard score.

After we gained the reputation for imaginative play calling at unexpected moments, we became even more effective.
Opposing defenses were no longer willing to expose themselves to a quick strike, so we reverted to our bread and
butter, Jim Taylor running off tackle.

My only regret was that the individuals who were as
responsible as any for our success during this time, our offensive linemen, seldom shared in the headlines.

Jim Ringo, our center, had long since forgiven me for the
beating his team took in 1953 when Alabama destroyed Syracuse in the Orange Bowl. The Packers drafted him in the
seventh round of their 1953 draft, and, with the exception
of an injury during his rookie season, he started every game
for the next ten years. He was undersize at six feet two and
230 pounds, but he was agile and smart. Jim had the knack
of using an opponent's size to his advantage. He was an
intellectual player, responsible for initiating our linemen's
calls at the line of scrimmage. He was also ahead of his time
off the field, but Lombardi didn't seem to appreciate this as
much as Jim did.

After the 1963 season Jim decided he deserved a healthy
raise. In previous years, his face-to-face negotiations with
Lombardi had not resulted in the type of pay increases he
was looking for. Jim was ready to straighten this out, so he
became the first player on our team to hire an agent.

Ringo's representative showed up in Lombardi's office
one day.

"Good morning, Coach Lombardi, I'm here to talk about
Jim Ringo's contract. I think he needs a substantial raise."

"Who are you?" asked Lombardi.

"Jim Ringo's agent."

"Wait just a minute."

Lombardi left the room and made a phone call. About
five minutes later, he returned and said, "I think Jim does
deserve a nice raise, but you're talking to the wrong person.
He's just been traded to the Philadelphia Eagles. Good-bye."

Although Lombardi was often curt with his comments,

he was also occasionally complimentary. He once called our right tackle, Forrest Gregg, "the finest player I have ever coached." I understood why.

Forrest had the ideal physical and emotional makeup for an offensive tackle. He was six feet four, 250 pounds, and could run like hell for a big man. More important, he was an intense competitor who had great concentration and tremendous pride. He never had a poor game; his blocking grades were consistently high.

Forrest was also versatile. In 1964 he stepped in for the injured Jerry Kramer and not only played well at guard, he made all-pro. He was a true fighter at any position.

With Forrest's success on the playing field came notoriety. Unfortunately, his running mate at tackle, Bob Skoronski, never received the recognition that he deserved.

Bob, perhaps more than any other player on our team, truly appreciated the opportunities his football career presented to him. His parents were first-generation Americans who worked in a rubber factory in Ansonia, Connecticut. They taught Bob the value of a strong family; he turned down a scholarship to Notre Dame and chose Indiana, because the Hoosiers offered a scholarship to his brother as well.

When he arrived as the Packers' number-five draft choice in 1956, I thought he might not be ready for professional football. As soon as he reached the dorm after returning from the college All-Star game, he left camp immediately. Bob dodged the entire fleet of Wisconsin state troopers, whom the Packers had alerted to look for our prize rookies, and drove back home to the East Coast. Those of us who wondered about Bob were dead wrong. He returned, started as a rookie, and, after a two-year stint in the military, developed into a valuable member of our line. Lombardi so appreciated his contributions that he named him offensive captain.

Bob wasn't flamboyant, but he was smart, alert, and aggressive. He was never outhustled. During a game against Detroit, Jim Taylor broke through the Lions' defense and chugged toward the end zone, which was more than 80 yards away. Out of the corner of my eye I saw number 76 come charging across the field to throw a block for Jimmy, about 40 or 50 yards from the line of scrimmage.

Bob had to overcome not only a lack of appreciation, but also the best pass rushers in the league. Defensive coaches generally line up their premier rushers opposite the offensive left tackle, Bob's position. They do so because a right-handed quarterback has his back turned to that area when attempting to pass. Bob was often my only line of protection from one of the best athletes on the opposing team. It is a tribute to him more than to me that I was able to concentrate on my receivers without worrying about being blind-sided.

Norm Masters, who logged plenty of playing time alternating with Bob, was an excellent player in his own right, and afforded us depth in the offensive line. Bob and Norm maintained an amicable relationship and encouraged each other to frustrate opposing defensive ends . . . except when we played the Bears. Chicago's defensive end, Doug Atkins, stood six feet eight, weighed 280 pounds, and could literally knock his opponents' helmets off with his huge hands. When Bob and Norm rotated, the first question always asked was, "You didn't do anything to piss off Atkins, did you?"

Our offensive guards, Jerry Kramer and Fuzzy Thurston, were, like our tackles, consistent and outstanding performers. And, as in their treatment of Forrest and Bob, the press focused most of its attention on one, Jerry.

Jerry is truly one of the remarkable stories on any team. The fact that he was an all-pro so many years is amazing, considering he was lucky to be alive.

When he was sixteen, he accidentally shot himself with a shotgun, nearly blowing his arm off. Undeterred, Jerry came even closer to killing himself a year later. In a freak accident, Jerry was chasing a calf when the calf stepped on a board, splintered it, and sent a chunk through Jerry's abdomen, nearly piercing his spine. No big deal. He later survived an operation to remove a grapefruit-size tumor, and then yet another, to remove several pieces of wood still lodged in his abdomen twelve years after the first operation.

For most people that would be plenty, but Jerry also managed to chop himself in the neck with an ax, suffer a serious case of blood poisoning, and shatter his ankle (during a game).

When he wasn't on his deathbed, he was making life miserable for defensive tackles. He was highly regarded when he arrived in 1958 and became even better during the next decade. Because of his personable, outgoing nature and good looks, he became a press favorite.

Jerry was the first to admit, however, that some of the praise being showered on him should have been reserved for our left guard, Fuzzy Thurston. Fuzzy didn't have to overcome the accidents Jerry did, but the odds were stacked against him nonetheless. In fact, Fuzzy may be the best example of what the Packers were all about.

Fuzzy attended college at Valparaiso University. That in and of itself is no big deal. But making the NFL was a very big deal—Fuzzy was the first player from that school to do so. Making the NFL after attending Valparaiso on a basketball scholarship can only be described as remarkable, particularly when we look at his path to Green Bay.

He was drafted by the Philadelphia Eagles in 1955 and later released. He joined the Bears . . . and was later released. He rejoined the Eagles and was released. He then played for the Colts before being traded to Green Bay. He was only six-one and 240 pounds, but obviously very determined.

On the playing field, he was a rotund stick of dynamite. His agility helped him become one of the best pulling guards in history, despite his lack of size. When I think of Fuzzy, though, I remember a game that was probably his most frustrating as a player but his greatest as a man. When Detroit spoiled our 1962 season by defeating us, 26–14, I was sacked eight or nine times, often by Roger Brown, the defensive tackle who lined up opposite Fuzzy.

Fuzzy's mother had died the day before the game. He never complained, never backed down, never alibied. He couldn't possibly have concentrated well, but Fuzzy was a true professional. He battled Roger all day and actually played better as we progressed. His display of courage was as great as any I had witnessed, until a few years ago, when he valiantly fought back against cancer of the larynx.

As our team basked in the glory of its second straight world championship, I was convinced that we were on our way to winning three in a row. Our players were healthy, in the prime of our careers, and avoiding off-the-field distractions.

On April 17, 1963, our title chances were dealt a terrific blow.

Paragraph 11 of the standard NFL player contract read as follows:

> Player acknowledges the right and the power of the Commissioner of the National Football League (a) to fine and suspend (b) to fine and suspend for life, immediately and/or (c) to cancel the contract of, any player who accepts a bribe or who agrees to throw or fix a game or who, having knowledge of the same, fails to report an offered bribe . . . or who bets on a game.

The previous August, before the start of the 1962 season, we heard some rumors that Paul was being investigated by the NFL for allegedly associating with gamblers, but we quickly dismissed them. Paul was our glamorous star, and this was probably just a case of someone trying to take a potshot at him.

In January, however, Commissioner Pete Rozelle summoned Paul to New York and confronted him with very serious and substantial evidence that Paul had wagered as much as $500 on NFL games. Paul did not deny the allegations.

On April 17 Commissioner Rozelle suspended Paul and Alex Karras of the Lions for betting on games.

Paul's teammates could hardly speak objectively about Rozelle's decision. Paul was our leader, a national celebrity. Our first line of defense on his behalf was the fact that he didn't bet on Packer games, but we understood the reasoning behind Rozelle's move. He had to preserve the integrity of the sport.

Lombardi was enraged. He constantly stressed the need to avoid distractions, and now his most visible player was creating a new headache. To Paul's credit, however, he went straight to Lombardi, admitted his mistake, and apologized. Lombardi said, "I hope you get reinstated next year, and I don't want you reporting at two hundred and thirty pounds. Stay in shape and out of trouble."

Most teams would have been somewhat discouraged over the prospect of playing an entire season without one of their most valuable assets. We weren't like most teams. When training camp began, Lombardi challenged us to overcome Paul's absence and repeat as champions.

We did not play as well as we had in the previous year, but we didn't fall on our faces, either. In fact, we won eleven games, lost only two, and tied one. Unfortunately, our two losses were to the Chicago Bears, who finished 11-1-2. Our 846 winning percentage may have been the highest ever recorded by any team that didn't participate in the playoffs.

Throughout the season, Lombardi urged us on to greater heights, often by referring directly to Paul: "No one person is bigger than this team."

After game six, he had to slightly modify his speeches. We traveled to St. Louis to play the Cardinals, and in the second half, we were driving for a touchdown. I dropped back to pass, but sensed a heavy rush and ran out of the pocket. As I was going out of bounds, Jim Hill, one of their defensive backs, swung at my head. I ducked but lost my balance, falling awkwardly on my right hand. Our team physicians told Lombardi that my broken hand would keep me out three or four weeks. Lombardi walked into the locker room and announced: "OK, now we've lost our quarterback. We'll still find a way to win."

We did.

Tom Moore and Elijah Pitts stepped into Paul's halfback position and played exceptionally well. Tom, in fact, made a number of all-pro teams.

Our backup quarterback, John Roach, replaced me and helped continue our winning streak. But Lombardi could not afford to play with only one quarterback, and obtained Zeke Bratkowski from the Los Angeles Rams.

We were intense rivals in college—Zeke was two years ahead of me at Georgia, one of Alabama's traditional enemies. I admired his passing and punting skills while he played for the Bulldogs and knew he would be a top-flight professional quarterback. The Chicago Bears thought so, too. They drafted him in 1954 with the expectation that he would develop into the NFL's next great quarterback. However, after his rookie season, he was called into active military duty and missed two years of development, while Ed Brown solidified his position as Chicago's signal caller.

When Zeke returned, he was very rusty and was played sparingly during the next four years. He finally got a break in 1961, when the Bears traded him to the Rams for Bill Wade, the Los Angeles quarterback. Zeke played regularly and well in 1961, but his good fortune quickly evaporated. Los Angeles drafted a tall, strong quarterback from North Carolina State named Roman Gabriel, and Zeke's playing time in 1962 shrunk.

Before Zeke had been in Green Bay more than an hour, he had accepted my invitation to come over to our house and review game films. I had been following this routine for years, but it was much more enjoyable with Zeke around to provide additional insight.

Zeke was joining a new organization under somewhat difficult circumstances, and he handled it remarkably well. He recognized the fact that I was the starting quarterback, but he was my biggest supporter, and became a very close friend.

His attitude was exemplary; he prepared himself for every game as though he would be playing all sixty minutes. Coach Lombardi quickly recognized that Zeke was going to be a valuable member of our organization and gave him the same amount of work during practice that I was allotted.

Our defensive unit especially benefited from Zeke's positive nature and team-oriented attitude. Zeke's "go team" was responsible for simulating the opponent's offense, and he gave our defense a great picture of what to expect. As a result, they were always extremely well prepared.

Zeke was consistently effective when called upon to replace me, but his analysis while I was healthy was equally important. I particularly remember a game against the Steelers in which we were struggling. Zeke was carefully studying the Pittsburgh defensive coordinator's signals to his players. He approached Lombardi.

"Coach, I think I've picked up their dog [blitz] signal."

"If you feel strongly about it," Lombardi said, "tell Bart."

At halftime, Zeke told me about his discovery. We were trailing 9–6, and needed any advantage we could get.

In the second half, I glanced over to our sideline after each huddle. When Zeke stood with his hands on his hips, I knew the Steelers would be blitzing. Zeke must have given me the signal five or six times, and we scored 35 points to win 41–9.

The frustration of finishing second to the Bears in 1963, despite a sterling record, lingered for months with many of the players and our coaches. The birth of our second son, Bret Michael, on February 1, 1964, spared me that dilemma. The thrill of being with Cherry during the delivery and actually witnessing the miracle of birth quickly put my life back into focus.

As the 1964 season approached, everyone on our team, our fans, the entire city, believed we would continue to dominate our opponents. We were deep at every position, we had Paul Hornung back, and we should have been hungry. However, the team's mood still seemed somewhat down, perhaps because we had missed the playoffs in 1963.

We played well, but inconsistently, and finished the season 8-5-1. The season is noteworthy only because we turned a 3-4 record into a respectable one by year's end. We lost only one game out of our last seven, and witnessed a commitment by Lombardi to bring in some additional skilled athletes during the off-season. The experts who wrote us off after the 1964 season were in for a shock.

# CHAPTER

# 9

After our first disappointing season since Vince Lombardi took control of the Packers, he developed a two-pronged attack to lead us out of our mediocrity and back to the top. The first step was a commitment on the part of the veteran players to regain the championship. Equally important was Lombardi's resolution to inject new blood into our lineup. This process began in 1964. Jim Ringo, Bill Quinlan, and Dave Hanner were replaced by Ken Bowman, Lionel Aldridge, and Ron Kostelnik, respectively. The retirement of linebacker Bill Forester and a trade involving Dan Currie gave way to Dave Robinson and Lee Roy Caffey. Lombardi also drafted tight end Marv Fleming and receiver Bob Long to provide greater depth at those positions. An improved Packer team was emerging.

Ken Bowman was a blue-collar athlete from the University of Wisconsin who was equal in size and toughness to his predecessor, Ringo. Bowman wore a harness to restrict the movement of his left shoulder during most of his ten-year career. The harness was designed to prevent his shoulder from repeatedly dislocating during game contact. It didn't always work, but Bowman somehow managed to miss only a few games. He attended law school during his years as a Packer and eventually received his law degree. He currently practices in the Green Bay area.

Aldridge was a bright, sensitive man, very articulate and possessed of the presence and voice to become a television commentator in Milwaukee. As a defensive end, he was not flashy, but a consistent performer.

Kostelnik was the son of a Pennsylvania coal miner and attended the University of Cincinnati, which was better known for basketball. He spent three years as a backup defensive tackle and then assumed a starting position in 1964 after Dave Hanner retired. Kos was light on his feet, very strong, and became a solid, dependable player. He was overlooked by everyone but his teammates.

Robinson and Caffey were imposing outside linebackers. Robinson, who weighed 245 pounds, and Caffey, 250, had agility as well as size. Dave, the Packers' first pick in the 1964 draft, was from Penn State University, where he had been an All-American. He also enjoyed reading Nietzsche (the German philosopher, not our linebacker). Robinson replaced Dan Currie, who Lombardi had traded to Los Angeles for receiver Carroll Dale after Robinson had proven himself early as a quality player.

Caffey was an "Aggie" from Texas A&M who joined the Packers via Philadelphia as part of the Ringo trade.

In the second month of the 1965 season, Lee Roy was forced to play middle linebacker against the Lions when Nitschke pulled a hamstring warming up before the game. He played as well in that game as he did the rest of the season and was selected, along with Robinson, to play in the Pro Bowl. Dallas' Tom Landry, when referring to the Packers' linebacker trio, said, "They may be the best ever."

The offense also benefited from the addition of Carroll Dale, the quick development of Bob Long, and the acquisition of tight ends Marv Fleming and Bill Anderson, who replaced Ron Kramer. Carroll had been a five-year starter with the Rams before his eight productive seasons with the Packers as one of my favorite targets. An All-American at Virginia Tech, Carroll had fooled defenders with his sneaky speed and ran very disciplined pass routes. He also possessed great hands and an outstanding work ethic. If Carroll lacked anything, it was more time to hunt grouse, his favorite hobby. He preferred the small-town atmosphere of Green Bay over Los Angeles. A devout man, he was an exemplary citizen and became a good friend.

Bob Long's path to professional football was unique. He had been a basketball player at Wichita State University and impressed pro football scouts on their visits to the Shockers' campus. Lacking the height to become an effective NBA player, Bob was persuaded to try football his senior year. Despite his lack of much college experience, the Packers drafted him in the fourth round in 1964 because of his speed and athletic ability.

Fleming was from the inner city of Los Angeles and the only black on the football team while attending the University of Utah. An eleventh-round draft choice, he became a frequent target for Lombardi's criticism. Lombardi knew that Marvin had the toughness to withstand it. In fact, Marvin appeared almost to thrive on it. He would smile, and perhaps Lombardi's criticisms made him reach even higher. Marvin accomplished something that no one else in the world has equaled—five Super Bowl appearances, two from his Green Bay tenure and three more from his experience with Miami.

Bill Anderson was acquired for a draft pick from the Washington Redskins during training camp in 1965. Although Bill was not the biggest man for his position at 225, he was a quality receiver and gained the starting position from Marvin late in the season.

There were also a pair of new faces in the defensive backfield. Bob Jeter replaced the retired Jessie Whittenton at right corner. Like Adderley, who played left corner, Bob was an offensive standout in college, a breakaway halfback at Iowa.

Also like Adderley, Bob was intended to be used as a wide receiver before being converted to defensive back. The Packers had selected Jeter in the second round of the 1960 college draft. Bob signed with the British Columbia Lions of the Canadian League, though. He played there for two years, and then sat out the '62 season before joining Green Bay in the fall of '63.

Safety Tom Brown's route to Green Bay was much more unusual. Tom, a great all-around athlete, went straight from the University of Maryland to major league baseball, joining the Washington Senators in the summer of '63. Since he had a school record of twelve interceptions his senior year, the Packers had hoped he would pursue a career in professional football, and drafted him in the second round before he began playing for the Senators. Tom changed his mind about baseball in 1964 and decided to give Green Bay a shot. In 1965 he moved ahead of our outstanding veteran Hank Gremminger at left safety.

The acquisition of Don Chandler, the talented veteran kicker of the New York Giants, was important to our team. Paul Hornung, for some mysterious reason, lost his rhythm as a placekicker during the '64 season, making fewer than one third of his field-goal attempts. He failed on five attempts in a game against Baltimore that we lost by three points, and a missed extra point turned out to be the decisive factor in a loss to the Vikings. Jerry Kramer, our alternate placekicker, was out of the lineup because of a near-fatal intestinal flareup caused by the slivers of wood that were discovered to have been lodged in his stomach. Chandler, who was not all that happy in New York, was contemplating retirement in '65 before the Packers acquired him for a late-round draft choice.

Don's NFL experience dated back to the period that Lombardi was coaching with the Giants, and Lombardi was very much aware of his kicking ability. Chandler, a combination punter and field-goal kicker, wasted little time convincing the rest of us. His 90-yard punt in a game early in the '65 season against San Francisco is still one of the longest in NFL history. He also demonstrated his reliability as a placekicker during three straight championship years.

After finishing second in the Western Division to the Chicago Bears in '63 and the Colts in '64, we were hungry to win it all in '65, and Lombardi was becoming impatient. After a grueling training camp we jumped off to a fast start with four straight victories, over Pittsburgh, Baltimore, Chicago, and San Francisco. In week five, we faced a strong Detroit team in a game of vital importance to our resurgence.

Going into the game, we were in first place, with the Lions and the Colts just one game back. At halftime the Lions held a comfortable 21–3 lead, however, and were threatening to tie us for first. Lombardi's halftime speech had a biting edge to it. Before we returned to the field, he calmly told the defensive players, "You are capable of shutting them out from here on. If you do it, we'll win, because we have made some slight adjustments offensively, and we're gonna make some big plays. But you've got to stop them."

We did just what Lombardi asked us to do. The defense shut out the Lions in the second half and I threw touchdown passes of 62, 31, and 77 yards to Bob Long, Tom Moore, and Carroll Dale. Late in the fourth quarter I took the ball in myself from 4 yards out to round out the scoring as we defeated Detroit, 31–21. It was one of the best halves our team had ever played.

When we faced the Lions again three weeks later, however, I had one of my poorest performances. Our 12–7 loss ended as my old friend Roger Brown, Detroit's 300-pound tackle, landed on me in our end zone for a safety and their eleventh sack of the game, an NFL record.

In the next-to-last game of the season we faced the Colts in a "must win" situation. A Colt victory would knock us out of the Western Conference title for the third consecutive year.

Dave Robinson made an interception in the closing seconds of the first half, turning the game around. We were in the lead by a slim 14–13 margin when Jimmy Taylor fumbled and Baltimore's Bobby Boyd scooped up the ball and returned it to our 3-yard line before he was knocked out of bounds. A 2-yard plunge by Colts fullback Jerry Hill put the ball on our 1, and it appeared the Colts would start the second half with the momentum as well as a six-point lead. As the rest of the Packer defense braced for another dive up the middle or a slant by halfback Lenny Moore, Robinson and Davis sensed something and, rather than taking a normal hard inside charge, came outside. They were right. Gary Cuozzo, substituting for the injured Johnny Unitas, attempted a flare pass to Hill.

As Cuozzo turned to throw, Davis was in his line of vision and forced him to loft his pass over Willie's outstretched arm. Robinson stepped in front of the Colt fullback and took off on an 87-yard jaunt before the swift Lenny Moore caught him at the Colts' 10-yard line. On the next play, with seconds remaining, I threw a touchdown strike to Boyd Dowler. Chandler added the extra point and we led at halftime 21–13, rather than trailing 20–14.

Approaching the end of his career, Paul Hornung had one of his most impressive performances. He accounted for nearly half of the 375 yards we gained offensively and scored five touchdowns, two of which were pass receptions of 51 and 65 yards. His effort and Robinson's interception were the keys to our 42–27 victory that day in Baltimore, which put us alone in first place of the Western Conference.

The San Francisco 49ers surprised everyone the last game of the season when they tied us, 24–24. Their entire team played exceptionally well, John Brodie in particular. The tie forced a playoff with the Colts, who had duplicated our 10-3-1 record. Since we had beaten the Colts twice during the regular season, we were given home-field advantage and the game was held in Green Bay. Going into the game, we had a distinct advantage—the Colts were without an experienced quarterback. Unitas was on crutches following midseason knee surgery and his backup, Cuozzo, was sidelined with an arm injury sustained in our game a few weeks earlier. Colts running back Tom Matte was converted to quarterback prior to their final game of the regular season. Although Matte had been a quarterback at Ohio State, he had virtually no experience in the position as a professional, which meant the Colts would have to rely heavily on their running game.

On the first play from scrimmage, we ran a fake draw play and I dumped the ball off to Bill Anderson in the left flat. Just as the ball arrived, Bill was hammered by Colt defender Lenny Lyles and the ball was jarred loose. Colts linebacker Don Shinnick snatched it in midair and headed down the sideline. I moved over to cut him off but Jim Welch met me first with a hard block. From the ground, I watched Shinnick cross our goal line. I struggled to my feet and was assisted off the field. On the sideline, I attempted to throw, only to discover that I could not lift my right arm above my shoulder. The collision with Welch had broken a rib. Fortunately, we had the NFL's best-prepared backup quarterback in Zeke Bratkowsi, and thus still maintained a distinct advantage over Baltimore at that position.

Zeke had the capacity to enter a game on short notice and lead our team without a hitch. In our second game of the season, against the Colts in Milwaukee, I was banged up in the third quarter and Zeke replaced me. He had noticed that the Colts were often running a weak-side rotation zone, and late in the fourth quarter called a play in which Max McGee came off inside and then broke outside the rotation toward the corner of the end zone. Zeke hit him perfectly for a 37-yard touchdown and the decisive score in our 20–17 victory.

A similar thing happened against the Vikings late in the season. Every game was crucial in our pursuit of the Western Conference championship. I sprained my right thumb during a pregame passing drill. I pulled away too quickly from center Bill Curry and the loose ball caught the thumb squarely on the end. Before we left the locker room for the opening kickoff, I told Zeke, "You better get ready." I played the first series and threw a touchdown strike to Boyd Dowler on an audible I called when the Vikings surprised us with a five-man front. My hand became so swollen, however, that I could no longer grip the ball. Zeke was excellent in relief, throwing touchdown passes to Carroll Dale and Bill Anderson. His 27-yard toss to Anderson occurred on a play he called at the line of scrimmage, and it won the game for us, 24–19. Those appearances against the Colts and the Vikings were virtually the only times Zeke played during the regular season. But he was physically and mentally prepared to perform at any time.

At halftime in the playoff game, the Colts had increased their lead to 10–0. Now it was my turn to assist. During our offensive meeting, we quickly reviewed the Colts' defensive approach. I reminded Zeke of some passes that should be better and reinforced his earlier successful choices. Zeke rose to the occasion and turned in an exceptional performance, connecting on twenty-two of thirty-nine passes for 248 yards. He threw a pass to Dale, who made a great catch on the Colts' 1-yard line to set up Paul Hornung's brief but productive run that yielded six points. Chandler added the extra point and the Packers narrowed Baltimore's margin to 10–7. Midway through the fourth quarter, Bratkowski led a Packer drive that put us in field-goal range near the Colts' 20 with 1:58 left to play.

With my ribs tightly taped, I took the snap from Bill Curry and spotted the ball at the 27-yard. As the ball approached the crossbar, it began to drift right. Don turned around and waved his hands in dismay, thinking our season was near the end. The backfield judge standing under the crossbar at the goal line, however, shot both arms in the air, signaling three points. This tied the game, 10–10. The Colts were outraged over what they felt was a missed field goal, but the game went into overtime.

Zeke led a drive that began at the Packers' 20-yard line following Lou Michaels' missed field-goal attempt from 47 yards. On fourth down with 13:39 elapsed in the overtime period, Chandler booted a 25-yard field goal. There was no question about this one; we had earned the right to face Cleveland for the NFL championship.

In the locker room after the game, a reporter asked me the inevitable question. "Bart, what about that kick?" he said. "How did it look to you?"

I had been in an excellent postion to watch the flight of the ball. "No doubt about it," I replied with a chuckle. "Besides, what else would you expect me to say?"

Later, Baltimore produced photographs that, they claimed, showed Chandler's field goal was wide when it sailed over the upright. This controversy resulted in the uprights being raised 20 feet above the crossbar the next year.

The Cleveland Browns were the defending world champions, having posted a 27–0 shutout over the Colts the year before. They continued to dominate the Eastern Conference in '65, winning the title by four games. As a result, they were favored to beat us on January 2, 1966, in Green Bay.

When my dad and I left the house to attend church early on the morning of the game, we found ourselves in the midst of a snowstorm. It was still snowing when we returned home. Cherry said to my dad, "Look at it out there. I don't see how Bart's going to throw the ball. You know it's going to affect the offense, but he didn't say a single word about the weather this morning."

I wasn't particularly interested in the weather. My ribs were of greater concern. I had not practiced very well during the week and found it difficult to adjust to being taped so heavily around my midsection. Although I was experiencing some pain, I knew that it would be diminished by a flow of adrenaline before kickoff. But I also realized that one clean blow to my ribs could force me out of the contest. The possibility that I might be unable to lead our team in such an important game troubled me.

I could sense Cherry's distress. As I walked out the front door of our home, I turned, gave Cherry a kiss, and said, "Honey, don't worry about it. You don't have to play today." It probably did very little to settle her, but I think it loosened Dad up a little.

The snow had a much more profound effect on the visiting Cleveland team. In an attempt to avoid the distractions of Green Bay's fast-paced night life, the Browns stayed in Appleton, a smaller city thirty minutes south of Green Bay. In doing so, they encountered a much greater distraction.

The road from Appleton was a mess. The highway department had somehow plowed the southbound lane by mistake, when the traffic was all going to be headed north, for the game. It took the Browns more than two hours to make the trip to the stadium, fighting the weather, slushy roads, and other traffic to the game along the way. Their late arrival allowed them only a brief pregame warm-up.

The snow had stopped by the opening kickoff, but the footing was soft and mushy, despite the fine job done by the Packers' ground crew. The conditions worsened when it began to rain, and the field turned into a muddy mess.

On our first possession, I went deep to Carroll Dale. I slipped just as I released the pass, and it was underthrown. Fortunately, Carroll slid to a stop, came back to the ball, caught it, and waltzed past the Browns' defensive back, who had fallen trying to adjust.

Don Chandler later added a pair of field goals, but the Browns scored twelve points to keep the game close at halftime, 13–12. We dominated the second half with our strong running game—Taylor and Hornung combined for over 200 yards. Our defense held the great Jim Brown to just 50 yards and prevented Cleveland's offense from scoring. Hornung's 13-yard touchdown run in the third quarter and Chandler's extra point, followed by a fourth-quarter field goal, resulted in a final score of 23–12. The Green Bay Packers were world champions for the ninth time, more than any other team in the history of pro football.

While the Packers brought national acclaim to the provincial northeastern Wisconsin city straddling the Fox River, Green Bay was generally isolated from the turbulence that was shaking the foundation of pro football by the emergence of the American Football League. Although it was initially labeled a second-class league, everyone was aware of the first-rate talent that it was managing to attract.

Team owners and coaches were making a concerted effort to secure the services of the best players in the game. The New York Jets signed Joe Namath, from my alma mater, Alabama, to a contract worth $400,000. Even before Namath's arrival in the AFL, there were a number of excellent quarterbacks performing in the new league, including NFL veterans George Blanda and Len Dawson, as well as an outstanding All-American from Kansas, John Hadl. In the spring of 1966, Al Davis, the aggressive coach of the Oakland Raiders, was named the AFL's commissioner, and he encouraged AFL teams to escalate their efforts to lure top talent from the established league. The Houston Oilers tendered a three-year offer of $870,000 to 49er quarterback John Brodie, who was reportedly making $70,000 a year. The Raiders had the Rams' Roman Gabriel committed to join their team and the Bears' tight end, Mike Ditka, was signed by the Oilers. (Brodie, Ditka, and Gabriel never played in the AFL, though, since the two leagues were to merge in the summer of 1966. They profited handsomely nonetheless.)

As the competition from the AFL in early 1966 continued to escalate, so did players' salaries. Collectively, the two leagues spent in excess of $7 million to sign athletes selected in the 1966 college draft. The popularity of the Packers in the mid-1960s was overwhelming; all of the games were sold out and the organization was profitable. Lombardi was not about to be outbid by the rival leagues for coveted high-round draft choices.

In that draft the Packers had three first-round selections. They obtained such a strong position not by chance but through beneficial trades and clever maneuvering by Lombardi and his assistants. The Packers' regular selection in the draft was Gale Gillingham, an impressive offensive lineman from Minnesota. Lombardi earmarked Gilly to take over for Fuzzy Thurston, who at thirty-three was nearing the end of his career.

Despite the fact that Gillingham was considered to be one of the premier offensive linemen drafted that year, the bulk of the media's attention was focused on a pair of highly touted running backs, Donnie Anderson of Texas Tech and Illinois's Jim Grabowski. Donnie was actually drafted as a "junior eligible" in 1965, on a choice we received from Philadelphia. Anderson, a unanimous All-American, was slotted to replace Paul Hornung, who also was approaching retirement. Like Paul, Donnie was a big versatile back and was as valuable as a receiver out of the backfield as he was running with the ball from scrimmage. He was also a fine punter and relieved Chandler of that responsibility in '67. Pat Peppler of the Packer staff signed him to a three-year contract in excess of $600,000 immediately following the Gator Bowl in Jacksonville, Florida, presenting Donnie with a bonus check for $70,000 as they stood beneath the goalposts. At the time, the total package was the largest ever offered to a first-year player.

The first-round selection that the Packers received from Detroit for Ron Kramer led to the acquisition of Jim Grabowski. The record-setting Grabowski had shattered Red Grange's career rushing mark at Illinois. As they had with Anderson, the Packers signed Grabowski to a three-year contract for a sizable sum, $400,000. Lombardi selected him to replace the legendary Jimmy Taylor, who had chosen to play out his option in 1966 and return to Louisiana. Lombardi believed that Taylor's decision was a breach of loyalty, and he hardly spoke to Jimmy the entire season.

Initially, it was not public knowledge that Taylor had decided to leave Green Bay. When an Associated Press reporter broke the story, Lombardi was infuriated. He felt that the privacy of the Packers had been violated and barred the reporter from our locker room. NFL commissioner Pete Rozelle stepped in, however, and the writer was allowed equal access. When the Green Bay Elks Club held a banquet in honor of Hornung and Taylor, Lombardi did not attend. He sent a written message praising Hornung and alluded to Taylor with a quote from Cicero about loyalty.

The veterans quickly accepted Anderson and Grabowski and made them feel welcome, despite their large price tags. In fact, many felt that the rookies' large salaries would eventually have a favorable effect on their own. I was one of many.

The large sums of money that were being offered never bothered me. I was making and enjoying a good living in

Green Bay. I also became involved in business activities that supplemented my compensation from the Packers. I became a member of a sports panel for Lincoln-Mercury, which featured golfers Arnold Palmer and Byron Nelson as well as tennis star Tony Trabert and Olympic champion Jesse Owens. I enjoyed working with them and my participation led to automobile dealerships in which, until recently, I was a partner.

As in the past, following our '65 championship I was afforded the opportunity to promote various products. I appeared in a television commercial for Bristol-Meyers, advertising their hair-care product Vitalis. The spot was first offered to Hornung, but the producer discovered Paul had a receding hairline. While filming the commercial, which called for me to throw a football through the opening of a moving tire, we encountered a bit of a problem.

Before filming I asked the director if it would not be better to completely cover the opening of the tire with paper, as opposed to having only one vertical strip and one horizontal piece of crepe paper, so the ball could be easily seen as it passed through the opening. The director assured me that the effect would be just fine the way the script was.

My first throw was a direct hit, passing right through the middle of the tire, but the cameraman said, "Hey, we didn't see a thing." We took a fifteen-minute break while crew members fastened strips of paper to the tire, completely covering the center. I resumed throwing, but after fifty attempts couldn't hit the opening from 20 yards. The crew was laughing hysterically. Just as the director was about to dub the scene with a stunt throw, I threw a crisp spiral that shattered the paper barrier. A cameraman shouted out, "Hey, Bart, one out of fifty ain't bad, but I hope your completion percentage is better next season."

The escalating player salaries and related raiding of talented players by the AFL persuaded the owners of teams in both leagues that a merger was essential to the stability of football. On June 8, 1966, a merger agreement was finalized.

At first, the regular-season schedule consisted of intra-league games only. The first-place finishers in each league would meet in January for the AFL-NFL world championship. The Packers, as reigning champions, were anxious to defend their title when training camp began in July '66.

Green Bay opened the regular season against Baltimore and Cleveland, two of our toughest rivals. We handled the Colts rather easily, beating them 24–3. In the second game, however, the Browns jumped out to a quick 14–0 lead. Following Cleveland's second touchdown, we had a fourth-and-1 situation on our 44-yard line. A field goal was out of the question and we needed a first down to continue a drive and keep the game within reach. We went for it. Cleveland was expecting a run all the way as I threw a play-action pass to Hornung, who was wide open down the left sideline. Paul ran untouched to the end zone for a 56-yard touchdown.

Late in the fourth quarter, we were again confronted with a crucial fourth-down situation. Cleveland was still leading, 20–14, and we had the ball on their 9-yard line with just over two minutes remaining. On fourth down, the Browns, knowing that we must pass, dropped seven men into the end zone and prevented me from throwing it there. I dumped it off on Taylor, who was flowing to the right at the line of scrimmage. Taylor carried the ball and Browns' defender Erich Barnes into the end zone. With Chandler's conversion, we had a thrilling 21–20 victory.

The Packers lost only two games the entire season. The 49ers nosed us out by one point in the fifth week and the Vikings surprised us with a three-point defeat in Green Bay. For some reason, we had trouble preparing ourselves mentally for the Vikings. Perhaps it was because we were always more concerned with the more established teams. The neighboring upstart Vikings, however, viewed us as their regional enemy and were always sky high.

We finished the season with a 12-2 record, three games ahead of the Colts. In the minds of many, the '66 Packers ranked with the '62 as being the best team in the Lombardi era. On an individual level, the '66 season represented the peak of my playing career. At age thirty-two, I was relatively injury-free the entire season and my completion precentage of 62.2 percent was the best in the league. I was particularly pleased with reducing my interceptions to three for the season, a career low. In addition, I felt honored to have been selected as the league's Most Valuable Player by a vote of NFL players. Murray Olderman presented me with the Jim Thorpe Trophy the day before the 1966 NFL championship game in Dallas.

The Cowboys, winners of the NFL's Eastern Conference, represented a serious obstacle to our effort to represent the league in the historic championship game against the champion of the AFL.

The forecast for Green Bay called for extremely cold weather in the week that preceded the conference championship game. As a result, Lombardi decided to give us a little break, and the team traveled to Tulsa, Oklahoma to prepare for the game. Unfortunately, we didn't travel far enough south. As luck would have it, we reached Oklahoma at the tail end of a snowstorm. When we went to the stadium of a local university to work out, the field was covered with snow and ice. If we needed a light moment, we received it after discovering a unique approach to snow removal. As we headed out for our first practice, we witnessed a young man driving a Cadillac with a bench tied to the rear bumper. As the week progressed, the weather improved dramatically and so did our workouts. We were extremely well prepared for Dallas when we left Tulsa.

Unlike in 1962 and 1965, when the weather affected the passing game, the long-range weather forecast for Dallas was good, and I was mentally prepared to play an outstanding game, knowing the Cowboys would work overtime trying to stop our running attack.

The championship game was held on a clear, 50-degree New Year's Day in Dallas, Texas. The Packers won the opening coin toss and elected to receive. On the game's eighth play from scrimmage, we capped a 76-yard drive when I tossed a 17-yard touchdown pass to Elijah Pitts.

Mel Renfro fumbled the ensuing kickoff when he was hit

hard by Dave Robinson. Grabowski, a rookie leader on our special teams, picked the ball up and returned it for a touchdown. It appeared as though the Packers were going to run Dallas right out of the Cotton Bowl. However, Dallas rallied quickly to tie the game, 14—14 at the end of the first quarter. On the second play of the second quarter, we regained the lead when I hit Carroll Dale for a 51-yard touchdown on first down. After trading field goals later in the second quarter, we had a 21—17 margin at halftime.

Dallas began the scoring in the second half with a 32-yard field goal by Danny Villanueva, but we moved ahead by eight with Boyd Dowler's 16-yard touchdown reception. Unfortunately, Boyd was injured at the end of the play as a result of Mike Gaechter's controversial (it was late and unnecessary) tackle in the Dallas end zone.

In the fourth quarter we had the ball on the Dallas 28-yard line, third down and 19 yards to go. The score was 28—20 and another touchdown would seemingly cinch the game. As we huddled, Max McGee, substituting for Boyd Dowler, whispered to me, "I can beat Livingston on a zig-out. Give me a shot." I nodded my approval. Max was always thinking. In our game preparation, we noticed that Livingston, Dallas' right corner, tended to overplay the middle on a post route. Lombardi and I had discussed taking advantage of it inside the Cowboys' 30. At the snap, Max cut to the middle and then broke to the outside. I couldn't believe how open he was when I threw to him for an easy score, my fourth touchdown pass of the day.

We should have wrapped up the game, but Cowboy defensive tackle Bob Lilly blocked Chandler's extra-point attempt, and our lead was only by 14. Dallas could now tie by scoring twice.

Five plays later, Meredith converted with Frank Clarke from 68 yards out and the Cowboys were within seven. With 1:52 remaining, Dallas had a first down on the Packer 2-yard line as a result of an errant punt by Chandler and a pass interference penalty on linebacker Dave Robinson.

Meredith handed the ball to his halfback, Dan Reeves,

who picked up a yard. On second down, the Cowboys jumped offside and our defense had some room to breathe. Meredith's pass to Reeves on second and 6 was bobbled and fell incomplete. On the next play, Meredith found Pettis Norman for a 4-yard gain before Tom Brown stopped him on our 2-yard line with forty-five seconds remaining.

The entire season for both teams was riding on the next play. Meredith rolled to his right on an option run-pass play. Dave Robinson broke through the line and chased him toward the sideline. Don, trapped against the sideline and in the grasp of Robinson, threw a desperation pass into the end zone that landed in the arms of safety Tom Brown. Green Bay had won the NFL title for the second straight year, 34–27.

A mechanical problem on our chartered jet forced Coach Lombardi to call an audible.

Rather than waiting at the airport, we returned to the hotel, where a beautiful buffet awaited us.

As Cherry, Mother, Dad, and I reached the ballroom level, we bumped into Bobby Layne, who was hosting a party for several friends in a suite on the twentieth floor. He insisted we join him. My mother and dad, who by now had become "teddy bears" for their two grandsons, and were affectionately called "Big Momma and Daddy" were thrilled with the invitation, since Bobby was one of their favorite players.

While chatting in his suite, I asked Bobby to tell my dad the story of a happening at the O'Hare Airport years before. Bobby did better than that. He quieted the entire room and began, "In 1961, several NFL quarterbacks and I had returned from a photo session in Chicago for *Life* magazine. We were having a few beers in a lounge at O'Hare, waiting for our planes to depart. From across the room, a lanky redhead spotted me and, weaving slightly, began calling my name as she moved closer. I looked up as she stopped about six feet away and said, "Get outa here, you're worse than third and three." If you think Bobby's guests howled, you should have heard the group of quarterbacks.

On the sidelines during a game, Coach Vince Lombardi was all business, studiously delivering comments to me, left, with Carroll Dale, center, and Zeke Bratkowski, partially hidden by the coach, taking it all in. *(Vernon J. Biever Photo)*

As I matured in Coach Lombardi's system, he gave me more authority. Here Lombardi scratches his head while he ponders my pointed suggestion. *(Starr family collection)*

The coach enjoys a light moment at training camp with his quarterback. He didn't often bare his molars on the practice field. *(Photo by George P. Miller)*

An early photograph of me and my brother, Hilton, in 1938. *(Starr family collection)*

A posed shot. My mom sent it to Dad when he was overseas in 1943. *(Starr family collection)*

My father, Ben Starr, wraps his arm paternally around his twelve-year-old son in front of our home in Montgomery, Alabama. *(Starr family collection)*

Nick Germanos, left, checks out the orange I'm holding on our arrival with the Alabama football team in Miami for the January 1, 1953, Orange Bowl. Our caps were the height of fashion. So were the pleated pants. *(Yeatman King)*

My coach at Sidney Lanier High School in Montgomery, Bill Moseley, points out the fundamentals of football to Bobby Barnes, left, and me. Coach Moseley was later my presenter at induction to the Pro Football Hall of Fame. *(Albert Kraus)*

During high school, as shown here, and through my first two years of college, I was a punter—until a back injury during kicking drills almost ended my career. (Albert Kraus)

My service as a second lieutenant in the air force lasted three and a half months in early 1957, after my rookie season with the Packers. *(Starr family collection)*

STARR BRYAN B 2LT
AO 3054111    5FEB57

My parents, Ben and Lula Starr, and son enjoy the Florida sun in Fort Lauderdale before Super Bowl II. *(Starr family collection)*

Bart Starr, Jr., at the age of six, takes a handoff from his father at his "office" on Lambeau Field. (Ralph H. Lewis)

The aches of Sunday are baked out Monday in the sauna at the Packer training quarters. Lying supine are tackle Bob Skoronski, top shelf, and linebacker Ray Nitschke, bottom shelf; to my left is Boyd Dowler; and Ron Kostelnik is to my right. (Photo by John E. Roemer)

Bob Skoronski, Elijah Pitts, and Chuck Mercein on the sidelines during a Packer game. (Vernon J. Biever Photo)

My father, Ben Starr, holds my game-day "ready" list and shares a victory
moment with me and defensive back Bobby Jeter after the Packers have won
the NFL title game at Dallas in 1966 and qualified for the first Super Bowl.
(Vernon J. Biever Photo)

Jerry Kramer, left,
locks hands with
Jimmy Taylor at a
Thousand Yard Club
dinner honoring
Jimmy at the Left
Guard restaurant,
owned by Fuzzy
Thurston, top right.
These were "the bet-
ter days," when Jerry
and Jimmy were
friendly. (Starr fam-
ily collection)

It was not your normal group shot when the 1962 Green Bay Packers assembled for their annual team photo. But it does include six players voted into the Pro Football Hall of Fame. They are Herb Adderley (26), in the center of the second row next to gap-toothed Dan Currie; Jim Ringo (51) and the quarterback who wore number 15, on the far left of the third row; Jim Taylor (31), in the middle of the top row; Willie Davis (87), just below him to the right; and Paul Hornung (5), top right. Note the double-team move Hornung and Dave Hanner (79) are putting on the late Henry Jordan (74). *(Photo by Bradley Photographers)*

After I became head coach of the Packers in 1975, I had statements made by Vince Lombardi printed and mounted at the top of the tunnel leading from the dressing room at the north end of Lambeau Field into the stadium. *(Vernon J. Biever Photo)*

Before tape came along to simplify the watching and study of football action, I became an expert at looping game film and spent countless hours with the projector in the basement of my home. *(Starr family collection)*

Before a play starts, it's the quarterback's job to make sure every player on offense is lined up in the correct formation, and to point if there are any adjustments to be made. I am reminding Paul Hornung that he needs to be moved up and to his right. *(Starr family collection)*

Hall of Famer Herb Adderley relaxes on the sidelines. *(Vernon J. Biever Photo)*

Willie Wood's unbeliev-
able athletic talent is no
secret. See his leaping
ability here! (Vernon J.
Biever Photo)

We called Willie Davis "Dr. Feelgood."
(Vernon J. Biever Photo)

All Pro linebacker Dave
Robinson in action.
(Photo by John E.
Biever)

This is a unique perspective on Bob Skoronski. (Vernon J. Biever Photo)

A passer must adhere to the basic mechanics of throwing the ball, including full extension and follow-through, disregarding everything around him, including the opponents. (Malcolm W. Emmons)

My single most famous moment—number 15 sneaking the ball over the goal line against Dallas in the closing seconds of the "Ice Bowl" on December 31, 1967, to win the game 21–17. Jerry Kramer (64) and Ken Bowman (57, hidden) have wedged out Jethro Pugh (75) of the Cowboys to give me room to get into the end zone. Linebacker Chuck Howley (54) is too late to stop me. Chuck Mercein (30) already has his arm raised to signal the touchdown. *(Photo by John Biever)*

Bob Schnelker, our brilliant coordinator on the right, ponders the next call with me during a timeout. David Whitehurst (17) stands by for the final decision. *(Vernon J. Biever Photo)*

Obviously, this wasn't one of our joyful moments on the Green Bay sideline. Paul Rudzinski, far left, holds a clipboard. John Meyer, the defensive coordinator, folds his arms impassively. Offensive line coach Ernie McMillan has the headphones on. The head coach is grim. Zeke Bratkowski, in charge of the quarterbacks, kneels. Behind him is assistant coach

Ross Fichtner. The identifiable players are linebacker Kurt Allerman (60), guard Derrel Gofourth (57), tight end Gary Lewis (81). *(Vernon J. Biever Photo)*

The family gathers poolside at the Summer Range Road house in De Pere. Bart junior, on the left, holds Shasta. My wife, Cherry, cuddles Panda. Bret holds down his father. *(Starr family collection)*

On a practice field in Green Bay with granddaughter Shannon. (The Milwaukee Journal *Photo*)

My parents celebrated their fiftieth wedding anniversary in 1982. With them, from left to right, are Bart junior, Martha, Cherry, and myself. *(Landmark Studios)*

A campaign swing took presidential candidate Ronald Reagan through Green Bay in 1979. I delayed practice thirty minutes to go out to the airport to greet him. *(AP Wide World Photos)*

At the 1984 reunion of the first Super Bowl team, which became the basis for a book by Jerry Kramer, we all donned our old jerseys at Lambeau Field and greeted fans at halftime. *(Vernon J. Biever Photo)*

I both played and coached in the Hall of Fame game at Canton, Ohio. And in the latter capacity, I visited the shrine with Cherry, and we stopped in front of the niche containing my bust and mural. *(Starr family collection)*

This was the famous trip to Hawaii in 1979 with Gary Knafelc and his wife, Emily. *(Starr family collection)*

# CHAPTER

## 10

Bill Anderson, our tight end, was, as usual, the last player to board the plane. Our chartered 727 was going to take us away from the frigid winter of Green Bay to balmy southern California as we prepared to play the Kansas City Chiefs in the AFL-NFL World Championship Game. California was two thousand miles away, but Bill was already sweating. He was terrified of flying.

Henry Jordan stopped by and said, "Hey, Anderson, hurry up. They've got a special seat waiting for you. It's on the wing."

Vince Lombardi was concerned about the distractions of Los Angeles, where the game would be played, so he arranged for us to practice at the University of California at Santa Barbara, about ninety miles north. As we circled over Santa Barbara in preparation for our landing, Bill suddenly blurted out, "Hey, he's not gonna try to land this thing on that runway? We'll never make it."

Henry, who was seated a few rows behind Bill, chimed in, "Sure we will. They land Cessnas here all the time."

While Henry took advantage of Bill's paranoia, several players struggled to get a look at the ground below.

Our final approach was uneventful until we touched down. The wheels had barely hit concrete when we were thrown forward, the pilot slamming on the brakes. Before the plane came to a stop, he quickly turned it to his left, and I could see we were at the end of the runway. Poor Bill almost passed out, and everyone, even Henry, was quiet.

At breakfast the following morning, Henry and I were eating oatmeal and eggs when Bill spotted us from the opposite end of the dining room. He shot toward us and practically hurdled a few tables in the process. Bill pointing to the morning newspaper that was clutched in his hand, said, "Jordan, you smartass, take a look at this."

About halfway down the front page, Henry and I both saw what Bill was referring to.

A headline read:

UNITED CANCELING 727 FLIGHTS

RUNWAY TOO SHORT, PILOTS CLAIM

AN ACCIDENT WAITING TO HAPPEN?

Henry refused to give in. "Bill, the real reason they're canceling those flights is because guys like you make the pilots nervous."

Bill shot back, "I didn't hear too much from you when we were burning rubber."

"All right, Bill, I give up. But I might as well tell you right now . . . Lombardi said that when we head back to Wisconsin, we're going to land at Clintonville."

A few hours later, we hopped on our bus and went to the practice field. The temperature was about 70 degrees and the humidity was nonexistent. We started running around the field like a bunch of kids. Lombardi was smiling from ear to ear.

Less than two weeks before, we had defeated the Cowboys in the Cotton Bowl, where the traditonal Bermuda grass was long and shaggy. By contrast, the field at the Santa Barbara stadium was one of the first to feature a new grass called Tifton Bermuda. The turf was closely cropped, soft, and very fast. After practicing for a week on the ice and mud in Green Bay, we welcomed the well-groomed field. Everyone felt fleet-footed and was very impressed with the new type of grass. During our first drill, I handed off to Jimmy Taylor, who roared through the imaginary defensive line and kept sprinting all the way to the goal line, about 70 yards away. Lombardi was delighted with our enthusiasm but afraid we might run ourselves to exhaustion. He finally had to literally order us off the field.

Lombardi always found a new way to motivate us, and this week was no exception. He challenged us on two separate, yet related, fronts.

First, he pointed out that we deserved to be there and needed to confirm that fact.

"Men, we are the best the NFL has to offer. We have won four NFL titles, damn near five, in seven years. We cannot afford to let down now."

In addition, he made it perfectly clear that the honor of the NFL was at stake. He treated this like a personal mission, and who could blame him? George Halas and Wellington Mara, highly respected members of the NFL's old guard, sent him telegrams wishing us well. They noted that the glory and tradition of the NFL was on the line and how proud they were to have the Green Bay Packers represent them. Lombardi was personally touched by the sentiment, but he also became tense and irritable. We could feel his sense of urgency as he told us, "There is no way—NO WAY—the Green Bay Packers are going to lose this football game."

We were highly confident we would win, but only because we believed in our abilities, not because we took the Chiefs lightly. In fact many members of the media stated that we appeared to be overly flattering in our remarks concerning the Kansas City players. Nonsense. Had those sportswriters seen the game films we had, they would have realized that our comments were genuine.

The burden of proof was squarely on our shoulders precisely because many people had dismissed the American Football League as a "Mickey Mouse" operation. Psychologically, the Chiefs were in a unique position. On the one hand, they didn't have to face the pressure we did, because a good showing on their part would be enough to quiet the critics. On the other hand, they lacked big-game experience. They had won one AFL title, while we had captured four NFL crowns. Their average age was twenty-six, ours twenty-eight. Their experience per player was five years, we had seven years under our belts. Only three of their athletes— quarterback Len Dawson, cornerback Fred Williamson, and placekicker Mike Mercer—had any background in the NFL.

Their pregame statements were somewhat tentative. Dawson, when asked whether Kansas City could actually win the game, replied, "If we can execute better, and . . . I think we can . . . we'll win. Yessir, we can run on Green Bay. We're counting on it."

Jerry Kramer summed up our feelings to Bill Wallace of *The New York Times*: "We've made a habit of winning. It's a matter of pride. We never consider the possibility of losing." We were not arrogant, just very confident.

Physically, the Chiefs certainly belonged on the field with the Packers, or anyone else for that matter. Their linemen in particular were larger than ours. Buck Buchanan, their defensive tackle, stood six feet seven and weighed 287 pounds. Offensive tackle Jim Tyrer was six-six and 292.

Linebacker Bobby Bell, running back Mike Garrett, Dawson and receiver Otis Taylor . . . all were fluid athletes who could play with anybody. Their only weakness, we felt, was their play at cornerback. Their defensive backs were not poor athletes, but their defensive strategy often left those players responsible for covering receivers with little help. Under those circumstances, the defensive backs must be exceptionally gifted, like Herb Adderley. To compound the problem, Kansas City liked to blitz their linebackers, which left their defensive backs even more vulnerable. Our receivers practiced especially hard that week, as they knew they would be seeing plenty of passes thrown their way.

Our workouts were crisp, our execution masterful. We were not particularly distracted by the pregame hype and we were able to concentrate on our task.

During the week leading up to the game, a number of sportswriters stopped referring to the contest as the AFL-NFL World Championship and started calling it the "Super Bowl." Lamar Hunt, the young owner of the Chiefs, had suggested the title at a league meeting the previous year, when plans for the game were being finalized. Still, it took some time before the name became semiofficial, and the phrase didn't exactly create a frenzy; the city of Los Angeles projected ticket sales of only 60,000 in the 100,000-seat coliseum.

We were pleased that we were able to focus on the game, and so were the reporters. There was no more coverage for our battle in Los Angeles than there had been in Dallas for our NFL title game against the Cowboys. I enjoyed having the opportunity to discuss the game with serious, talented writers like Will McDonough, a young reporter from the *Boston Globe*. When we visited in the hotel lobby, I was impressed with the amount of background work he had done. He was all business.

Fred Williamson of the Chiefs, on the other hand, was all mouth. He took advantage of the national exposure to fire out one outrageous statement after another. He was a hard-hitting defensive back who had nicknamed himself "The Hammer."

His first task was to make sure every fan knew why his calling card was appropriate. He described the karate blows he was going to deliver to any Green Bay receiver who dared to enter his turf.

Henry Jordan approached Max McGee and said, "Max, you're lucky you probably won't be playing . . . 'The Hammer' is looking for blood."

Max laughed. "Hell, he's nothing but a cheapshot artist. I'll be sure to warn Carroll and Boyd."

Williamson then proceeded to insult about half our players. He was particularly rough on Jimmy Taylor, whom he said, "Would have been no big deal in our league. Jim Nance [of the Boston Patriots] runs a lot harder."

Perhaps The Hammer thought we would become concerned after reading about his remarks. We were nothing more than amused. We ran down to the newsstand every morning so we could have a good laugh along with our breakfast.

We did respect Williamson's skills—he was intelligent and strong, but he gambled a little too often and left himself vulnerable to the big play.

The national television networks loved the attention Fred was getting. Both NBC, which broadcast the AFL games and CBS which televised NFL clashes, would be carrying the game. They needed all the hype anyone could muster, because they had paid $1 million each for the television rights and had to convince advertising executives that $70,000—$80,000 per minute was not too much to pay. The ticket prices for the game were just as outrageous—$6, $10, even $12 per seat.

On the morning of our game, I woke up, took a quick shower, and headed downstairs to read the paper and have some breakfast. As I strolled through the lobby, I walked by Max McGee and greeted him, "Good morning, Max." He looked like he might need a shave and was wearing the same sports coat and slacks as the night before. Max said, "Hey, Bart," glanced at his watch, and quickly headed for the elevators.

Max had met a cute little blonde from Chicago, and now, five hours before kickoff, was returning for a couple of hours of sleep.

We were thirteen-point favorites as Willie Davis and Bob Skoronski, our captains, greeted Kansas City's Jerry Mays and Jon Gilliam at midfield for the coin flip. Lombardi was not excessively superstitious, but he believed the eagle on a silver dollar made the tails side heavier. Willie called heads and we won the toss. Despite a crowd of only sixty-three thousand, both teams were ready. No one could have possibly guessed who the hero would turn out to be, however.

During our first series, Boyd Dowler crashed to the turf and sprained his right shoulder. Max was sitting on the bench, catching up on his rest. It didn't last long.

"McGee!" shouted Lombardi.

Max thought to himself, Damn, he must have found out about last night. He ran over to Lombardi, prepared for the worst.

"What is it, Coach?"

"Max, Dowler just hurt his shoulder. Get in there."

As Max jogged toward our huddle, I could hardly believe my eyes. He looked ready to go. Max always had the ability to turn his humor and concentration on and off, but this was an extreme example even by his standards. A few years earlier, he had helped break the tension of a close game in Los Angeles when, after dropping a sure touchdown pass, he returned to the huddle and said, "God, the smog's thick today." On this occasion, however, he knew what was needed and was dead serious.

After exchanging punts, we took over at our own 20 and quickly moved downfield on pass receptions by Marv Fleming, Elijah Pitts, and Carroll Dale. Then Max took over. On third and 3 from the Chiefs' 37-yard line, I dropped back to pass. Just as I prepared to throw the ball to Max, who was running a short post route, Buck Buchanan crashed through our line. I shuffled to avoid the pressure from Buchanan but he hit me before the ball left my hand. The contact affected the velocity of the ball and caused it to head right at defensive back Willie Mitchell, who was about a yard behind Max. However, in full stride, Max reached back with his right hand, stabbed the ball, pulled it in, and raced untouched into the end zone.

After Don Chandler kicked the extra point to make the score 7–0, I trotted off the field and congratulated Max.

"Hell of a catch, Max," I said.

"Made it look easy, didn't I?" he laughed.

"Max, I've got to tell you, I was surprised you caught that thing."

Max replied, "You think *you* were surprised. I was just

sticking my hand out to keep Mitchell from picking it off. I looked back and there was the ball in my hand, so I kept running."

Kansas City didn't exactly fall apart after witnessing Max's heroics. As a matter of fact, they immediately drove to our 33, but missed a 40-yard field goal. Following a couple of misfires on my part, they drove 66 yards for a touchdown to tie the game. We were in a real ball game. We knew it and the Chiefs knew it.

Kansas City kicked off and we quickly picked up 9 yards on two running plays. Faced with a third and 1 from our own 36, I decided to go for the home run. I faked a handoff to Jimmy Taylor and hit Carroll Dale for a 64-yard touchdown. My favorite play, a short-yardage bomb, had worked like a charm. Well, almost a charm. The officials called an illegal procedure penalty, and we had to start all over again. We were undaunted. This drive would probably determine whether Kansas City would have the opportunity to take the lead going into the halftime. Their defense was pumped up, aggressive. They forced us into four third-and-long situations, but we responded every time with a completion. On first down from their 14, Jim Taylor swept to his left, cut sharply upfield, and barreled into the end zone. Considering the adversity of having a score nullified, the quality of our opponent, and the pressure of the game, that drive was one of our best all season.

Once again, however, the Chiefs bounced right back and drove downfield, this time for a field goal just before the second quarter ended.

We had played hard in the first half, but no one seemed to be relaxed, except for Max, of course. Lombardi was composed, direct, and concise in his comments.

"We've looked at them for a half," he said. "We know what they're trying to do. Defense, let's take control of the game. Get more pressure on Dawson and create some opportunities for the offense."

The Chiefs took the opening kickoff of the second half and quickly drove to their 49. It was third and 5, a big, big play. As it turned out, it was the biggest.

Dawson dropped back and, under a heavy rush, threw quickly toward Fred Arbanas, their tight end. But before the ball arrived, Willie Wood stepped in front, intercepted, and returned the ball to the Kansas City 5-yard line.

It was an ideal opportunity to cross up the Chiefs' defense. I figured they'd be looking for Jimmy Taylor again, and they were. Elijah Pitts took the handoff and scored easily. The game, for all intents and purposes, was over.

Late in the third quarter, we mounted another sustained drive that dashed any hopes of a Kansas City comeback. On a first-down play from their 13, I fired a perfect strike to Max in the end zone. This time, he nearly dropped the easy pass, bobbling it for a few strides before hauling it in.

The fourth quarter of our game was uneventful, with one notable exception. We finally nailed The Hammer. I mean really nailed him. Gale Gillingham, our powerful left guard, led Donny Anderson on a sweep around the right end. The Hammer, ever aggressive, came up to meet Gillingham, but Gilly just ran right over him. Gilly's knee caught The Hammer flush on the helmet, Donny tumbled over both of them, and The Hammer went down and out for the count.

After our 35–10 victory, Lombardi was asked whether the Chiefs were comparable to some of the top NFL teams.

He replied, "No . . . there are several teams in our league that are better than they are."

Lombardi's response was simply impulsive. Later, after he had the chance to reflect and review the game films, he was more gracious. Coach Lombardi and I attended a couple of post–Super Bowl banquets together, and he was highly complimentary of the Chiefs.

The entire Packer team felt the same way. Kansas City had an excellent team and many of us believed that they would be good enough to win it all after their team matured a little.

Ironically, our triumph was extremely poignant for all of us. Paul Hornung, our Golden Boy, was hampered by a pinched nerve in his neck and never appeared in the game. We knew that he might never again play for the Packers, and I couldn't help but feel badly for him as we celebrated in the locker room. His buddy, Max McGee, played a remarkable game, but Paul could only watch.

He retired before the next season began.

Paul's longtime running mate, Jimmy Taylor, had also played his last game for Green Bay, although he was able to make a major contribution in it. He became a free agent following the season, signed with the New Orleans Saints, and played with them for one full year before retiring.

After the game, I was chosen the Most Valuable Player of Super Bowl I. The award didn't mean nearly as much, however, as Lombardi's postgame statement:

"I don't know where the story began that Bart couldn't throw the long pass. That's ridiculous . . . he can throw with anyone. He's a fine quarterback, and I'm delighted that he's finally getting the recognition he has long deserved."

Had I been able to vote for the MVP of the game, I would have chosen Max. He caught seven passes for 138 yards and two touchdowns, but more important, he set the tempo for our passing game. The award is given to the Most *Valuable* Player, and had Max not stepped in for Boyd and played so well, our offense might have struggled.

At the postgame party Lombardi was smiling and couldn't help getting in a little jab at Max.

"McGee," he said, "I can't figure you out."

"How's that, Coach?"

"I've been coaching you for eight years, and I've never seen anyone like you. You're a hell of a receiver, but you drive me nuts. You make a circus catch of a pass thrown three feet behind you, then you turn around and drop one that hits you right in the numbers."

Max paused for a moment, then put his arm around me and smiled.

"Coach," he said, "it's easy to explain. I haven't had much practice catching ones thrown right to me."

About six or seven of the Packers still had one more game to play that year—the Pro Bowl—and the praise we received continued that week as well. George Allen, the head coach of the Los Angeles Rams, would be leading the Western

Conference stars against the finest players from the East. He called for a meeting at nine o'clock on the morning after the Super Bowl. He probably didn't expect the Packer representatives to be on hand for the initial meeting. We not only showed up, we were some of the first to arrive.

When Allen entered the meeting room, he was pleasantly surprised to see us waiting for him, and saluted us.

"I think the finest tribute I can pay the Green Bay Packers is to point out to you people . . . their spirit of teamwork, of caring for one another. They've just won the biggest event in pro football history, but now that game is behind them and they recognize their obligations to be here for one more game. Every one of them is here."

Vince Lombardi's players wouldn't have been anywhere else.

Allen's praise for us didn't prevent him from naming John Unitas to start at quarterback, just as Lombardi had following the 1962 season. I could understand Lombardi's reluctance to start all his players four years before, but Allen's decision really ticked me off.

John Unitas was one of the greatest quarterbacks in the history of professional football, and also a friend. I had great respect for him. In 1966, however, I was the National Football League's MVP in the regular season and the Super Bowl. Our record was 12-2, and we came close to going undefeated, losing two games by a total of four points. We beat Baltimore twice during the season.

However, Allen decided to start Unitas in the All-Star game. Though his decision was frustrating, I thoroughly enjoyed working with George in practice the week prior to the game. I was very impressed by the seriousness of his approach and the effort he made to prepare the team. The trouble that he went to in an attempt to gain an edge for his team's quarterbacks and receivers was particularly impressive.

He had a reel of film compiled that showed the East team's cornerbacks covering receivers of the West team in various games from prior years. The film man must have had a heck of a time piecing it together, as there were clips from forty or fifty different games.

On the morning of the game, Allen saw Cherry standing at the front desk of the hotel.

"Cherry, what are you doing?" asked George.

"I'm checking out and going home," answered Cherry.

"Why?" he inquired.

"Because Bart isn't starting and I'm not interested in sitting in the rain to watch someone else play."

George was truly concerned and tried to reason with her. "Cherry, I'm not starting Johnny because he had a better year than Bart; I'm starting him because I thought Bart would enjoy not having to worry about the game. He just finished playing the biggest game in years."

Cherry smiled and said lightly, "Coach, I'm not going to hold a grudge. I like you very much and so does Bart. But I want you to know, Bart has a memory like an elephant."

# CHAPTER

## 11

The Packers of my time were most dominant during the 1962 and 1966 seasons, but 1967 was arguably the most rewarding season for the fans, the players, and Lombardi.

The challenge was monumental. No team in the modern history of professional football had won three consecutive world championships.

The obstacles were formidable. Our team was breaking up, and the remaining veterans had, for the most part, seen their best years.

We had one reliable factor, however—Vince Lombardi. The 1967 season would not only be our greatest test, but his as well.

It didn't take long for me to realize that things were going to be more difficult this year—I threw more interceptions in our first game, against the Lions, than I had the entire previous year. Lombardi knew that I was hurting going into the game with shoulder and rib injuries; he was not only not harsh in his comments to me, he was complimentary. And to the surprise of no one, we were able to overcome four turnovers and a 17–0 halftime deficit, as we rallied to tie the Lions, 17–17.

We hosted the Bears in week two, and I decided to go ahead and get most of my interceptions out of the way for the whole season, firing five passes to the wrong colored jerseys. Our defense, however, limited Chicago to just six first downs as we defeated Chicago, 17–13. More important, the fans witnessed the emergence of our bonus babies—Jim Grabowski and Donny Anderson—as exciting young stars. Grabbo led the team in rushing and was on his way to a superlative season before a knee injury cut him down. Anderson contributed in a number of ways—running, catching, throwing, even punting. His left-footed spirals didn't travel all that far, but his hang time was excellent and his reverse spin created nightmares for opposing punt returners.

Lombardi continually stressed the need for everyone on the team to forget our egos and concentrate on team goals. Fuzzy Thurston listened better than anyone. He had already lost his starting position to young Gale Gillingham, but Fuzzy constantly pushed, coached, and praised Gilly. Fuzzy's actions were a perfect example of how our team remained a cohesive unit.

The third game of the season was a thing of beauty for our fans, as we shut out the Atlanta Falcons, 23–0. It wasn't exactly my favorite game, however. Midway through the first quarter, Tommy Nobis, the Falcons' version of Ray Nitschke, nailed me with a clean shot shortly after I threw a pass. When I landed on my right shoulder, it tore apart inside. That injury caused me to miss our next two games and would ultimately lead to my retirement.

Midway through the season, we traveled to St. Louis to play the Cardinals. They took a 23–17 lead in the fourth quarter before we sprang the "Road Runner" on them. Travis Williams, a rookie from Arizona State, was a big man (215 pounds) with blazing speed. Having been coached by Frank Kush, he was used to tough camps and discipline, but he had yet to adapt to our offensive system. As the Cardinals prepared to deliver the knockout blow, Lombardi decided to send Travis back to return his first kickoff for the Green Bay Packers.

Travis gathered in Jim Bakken's kickoff at the 7-yard line, burst through a small gap, and turned on the afterburners. His 93-yard return stunned the Cardinals, silenced the crowd, and turned the game around, as we won, 31–23.

Travis was just warming up. Two weeks later, we hosted Cleveland in Milwaukee. The Browns' coach, Blanton Collier, was determined to stop Travis at any cost—he even went so far as to keep two coverage men back as "safeties" in case Travis took off. Travis liked a tough challenge, however. Before the opening kickoff, he said to Gale Gillingham, Travis' lead blocker, "Come on now, Gilly, I feel good. I'm gonna run one back today."

Travis was wrong—he ran back two, on consecutive attempts, one for 87 yards, one for 85. Cleveland had a good team—they finished the season 9-5—but they were shell-shocked. We killed them, 55–7.

For the season, Travis set an NFL record for most kickoff returns for touchdowns, four. He also established a standard that makes all others pale by comparison—he averaged 41.1 yards per kickoff return. To put that in perspective, the old mark was 35.2, so Travis increased that average by almost 17 percent. No one has come close since, and I doubt if anyone ever will.

In addition to the changes brought about by our newcomers, the National Football League made a structural change. Each conference was now divided into two divisions, with the division winners scheduled to meet in a playoff before taking on the other conference champ. We clinched the Central Division crown with a 17–13 victory over the Bears in Game 11.

We still had three to play, but, with little motivation left before the playoffs and liberal substitution of younger players, we stumbled through them, losing two and nearly blowing one to the Vikings. In the next-to-last game of the season, we lost to the Rams in the last minute after they blocked a punt. Lombardi was beside himself with anger. After the game, he alluded to a possible playoff rematch with this comment: "They won't beat us the next time."

In the last week of the regular season, the Rams hosted the Colts, who were undefeated. After a 34–10 shellacking, Los Angeles was awarded the Coastal Division title because they had a better head-to-head record, although they each finshed 11-1-2. The Rams then flew to Milwaukee to play us for the Western Conference championship.

When they arrived, the hotel manager delivered a note to George Allen. It read:

Dear Coach Allen,
    Remember what I told you. Bart never forgets.
                                Cherry

As a matter of fact, revenge was the farthest thing from my mind. I had plenty to worry about already as we prepared to host a Ram team that had been labeled the "new powerhouse in the NFL." Their defensive line, "The Fearsome Foursome," featured two of the greatest linemen in NFL history, Deacon Jones and Merlin Olsen.

Merlin was one of our most respected opponents, combining awesome strength and agility with consistent effort. He was also one of the classiest players we faced at any position.

As great as Merlin was, Deacon was the player we feared most. All season, he had disrupted offenses with his ability to rush the passer. Our game plan was designed specifically to neutralize him. First, we lined up our tight end, Marv Fleming, opposite Deacon for most of the game. Marv and Forrest Gregg, our right tackle, double-teamed him play after play. We used this blocking scheme on running plays and quick rhythm passes, so Deacon wouldn't be able to tee off at any time.

Lombardi was pleased with the way we executed offensively, and ecstatic over our defensive performance. After a first-quarter scoring pass by Roman Gabriel, the Rams were barely able to move the ball all day. Of course, we were motivated by pride and by our pocketbooks. After our 28–7 victory Henry Jordan said, "No question about it, I was playing for the money. I have an expensive wife." Lombardi, however, was closer to tears than to laughter. He was so overwhelmed with emotion he could hardly talk. He knew we had overcome injuries, changes, and one hell of an opponent to get this far. All season, he heard we were too old, unable to play Packer football the way we used to. Now, as coach of the Western Conference champions, he could only manage to say, "I'm extremely proud of you . . . great effort," before he broke down.

As Lombardi left for media interviews, I looked around and sensed we wouldn't be playing for him much longer. The probability of his retirement was not discussed, but it was thick in the air. Meanwhile, the team was committed to winning the championship for him.

Our victory over the Cowboys eight days later in the "Ice Bowl" drained us emotionally as well as physically. The previous year we had been taken to the wire by Dallas, and we knew going into the game that they would be ready for us. We considered it our championship game and didn't give a thought to Super Bowl II. After our frigid victory, the last thing I wanted to do was play another football game.

Following the AFL and NFL championship games, Johnny Carson invited the quarterbacks from the participating teams to appear on The Tonight Show. The taping of the show was scheduled for the Monday following the games, and I was also scheduled to participate in a Tuesday luncheon for Sports Illustrated. As a result of my involvement with the luncheon, Sports Illustrated made my and Cherry's hotel arrangements.

The Tonight Show handled the arrangements for the other three quarterbacks—Daryle Lamonica, Don Meredith, and Pete Beathard. When we arrived in New York, we could not believe our accommodations—the presidential suite at the New York Hilton. The suite was as big as our home in Green Bay.

On Monday afternoon our itinerary called for all of the quarterbacks to meet at our hotel before going to dinner, and later, to the television studio. Meredeth was the last to arrive. After glancing around our suite, he said with his Southern drawl, "Gawd damn . . . I'd heard winnin' has its rewards, but this is ridiculous."

Our opponents in Miami were the Oakland Raiders, who, like the Kansas City Chiefs, were thirteen-point underdogs, but who, also like the Chiefs, possessed some outstanding talent, including receiver Fred Biletnikoff, center Jim Otto, defensive back Willie Brown, rookie guard Gene Upshaw, and quarterback Daryle Lamonica.

The Raiders' version of "The Hammer" was Big Ben Davidson, a six-foot-seven-inch, 265-pound defensive end with a flourishing handlebar moustache. His reputation as a fearsome competitor had been enhanced during the regular season, when he broke Joe Namath's cheekbone. But we knew better. Ben played with us briefly in 1961, and we remembered him as a gentle man with a gruff voice.

The man on the Raiders who attracted much of the media's attention, however, was their managing general partner, Al Davis. He overshadowed Davidson, Lamonica, and coach John Rauch, and with good reason: He was building the Raiders much the way Lombardi had the Packers, with smart draft choices and players who didn't fit within other organizations. When asked to sum up his team's chances, he replied, tongue in cheek, "Why, can you even imagine us on the same field as the Green Bay Packers?"

The Green Bay Packers were unable to picture themselves on any field, as it took us quite a while to thaw out from the Dallas game. Unlike the enthusiasm we'd brought to our workouts in Santa Barbara the year before, we really had to work at getting "up" for what was now the biggest game of the season. We did have a tremendous advantage in having already played in a Super Bowl, but the Raiders were hot—they lost only one game all year—and ready to win.

Lombardi's demeanor in the days preceding the game was our team's most dramatic change from Super Bowl I. He was no longer uptight and ornery, but rather relaxed and cheerful. He even broke a longstanding tradition and allowed our wives to accompany us on the trip. During the "Five O'Clock Club" cocktail sessions with the media, he was jovial and informative, with one major exception.

Rumors had been circulating for weeks that Lombardi was going to retire from coaching after the game and remain as the general manager. Although he refused to discuss the subject, United Press International carried a quote from him in which he said, "I haven't decided yet. I do know that in pro football today it is almost impossible to be both coach and general manager if you want to do well at either."

He mentioned nothing about his possible retirement to us but we couldn't help but think about it.

On the Thursday morning before the game, Lombardi walked into a large conference room in the hotel where the team had been assembled prior to our separate offensive and defensive group meetings. He stood in front of the team briefly and then began a short speech that recapped our season. He talked about the numerous injuries that had troubled the team and how we had overcome them as well as other adversities. He mentioned how well we had responded to the pressure of competing for a third straight championship. Then, suddenly, he began to choke up as he said, "I want . . ." He paused and his voice cracked as he continued, "I just want to tell you how very proud I am . . . of all of you." Then, in an abrupt change he said gruffly, "Defense down the hall . . . let's break up," and walked out into the hallway. After the defensive players had filed out of the room, he returned, turned the lights off, and flipped on the film projector without saying another word.

The concept of a Super Bowl was no longer novel, but we noticed that the fans in Miami were much more excited than those in Los Angeles; the Orange Bowl was sold out and a large chunk of the crowd was comprised of Packer fans who had chartered ten planes from Wisconsin.

On the game's first play, Ray Nitschke stopped a Raiders sweep cold, and we quickly forced them to punt. After two field goals from Don Chandler, we had possession of the ball from our own 38-yard line. In the huddle, I called "Flood Six Wing Square Out." The "Wing Square Out" meant that Carroll Dale, the primary receiver, would be running a deep turnout to the sideline. "Flood Six" was a built in blitz audible, meaning that I would throw toward Boyd Dowler if Oakland blitzed.

They charged full bore, and when I saw them coming, I looked for Boyd. The Raider defensive backs, Willie Brown and Kent McCloughan, used the "bump-and-run" technique, playing close to the wide receivers and trying to knock them off stride. McCloughan picked up Boyd as he came off the line of scrimmage and stayed with him for 8 or 9 yards, then dropped off. The Raiders free safety, Howie Williams, was supposed to pick up Boyd, but blew the coverage. I threw a pass that hit Boyd in full stride, and he galloped to the end zone to complete the 62-yard touchdown.

Oakland briefly rallied to cut our lead to 16–7, but we scored ten points to put the game away. After our 33–14 victory, Jerry Kramer and Forrest Gregg carried Lombardi off the field on their shoulders.

# CHAPTER

## 12

Lombardi continued to dodge questions about his future. But on February 1, 1968, he finally announced what we already knew. He read from typed notes. "Because of the emotion involved, I felt I could not trust myself to say what I must say unless it was written," he explained. His announcement concluded, "Gentlemen, let me introduce to you the new head coach of the Packers . . . Phil Bengtson."

Lombardi's retirement prompted me to contemplate my own. After having won three straight world championships, including two Super Bowls, it was the perfect time to go out on top. However, at thirty-four I still enjoyed the game immensely. More important, Lombardi's replacement, Phil Bengtson, had been an integral part of our success and I felt that the veteran players owed him their support.

The team was obviously still rich with talent, albeit much older, but the ball just didn't seem to bounce our way in '68. We lost four games by less than a touchdown and finished with a 6-7-1 record. It was our first losing season in ten years. The Vikings won the division with an 8-6 record behind a dominating defensive line that featured Alan Page, Carl Eller, and Jim Marshall and the talented Fran Tarkenton at quarterback.

In '69 we had a more respectable finish at 8-6, but Minnesota ran away with the division at 12-2.

The '68 and '69 seasons were certainly disappointing ones for the team and fans alike. For me, they were not only disappointing but extremely frustrating, as I was repeatedly injured. First, I separated the cartliage in my ribs and later broke several of them. I also suffered a concussion and was bothered by chronic soreness in my right shoulder.

I continued to lead the league in passing efficiency with completion percentages of 63.7 and 62.2 during the '68 and '69 seasons respectively. However, I missed twenty-eight quarters of action in Bengtson's first year as head coach and twenty-seven in his second. I also began to miss some of my former teammates.

Fuzzy Thurston, Don Chandler, and Max McGee retired following Super Bowl II, and Bob Long traveled to the Falcons. A season later, Jerry Kramer, Bob Skoronski, Ron Kostelnik, Tom Brown, and Zeke Bratkowski hung it up. Following them at the end of the '69 season were Willie Davis, Henry Jordan, and Boyd Dowler. In addition, Marv Fleming was traded to the Dolphins and Herb Adderley to the Cowboys while Lee Roy Caffey left to play for the Bears. Finally, the 1970 season was the last in a Packer uniform for Bob Jeter, Forrest Gregg, and Jim Grabowski. Altogether, eighteen key players had disappeared in a three-year period.

With the exception of an occassional flareup of my sore shoulder, I was relatively injury-free during 1970 and played most of the season. I encountered a new experience in the opening game of the '70 season, one we lost to Detroit. I was booed while returning to the sidelines after throwing an incomplete pass on third down. As disappointing as the experience was, I could not blame the Green Bay fans. They had become accustomed to the Packers' domination in the championship years and were only voicing their displeasure

over our more recent medicore performances. On the other
hand, one of the most memorable and gratifying experiences
of my life took place during the same season. The Packer
organization designated October 18, 1970, as Bart Starr Day,
in honor of my accomplishments. The evening before our
game against the Los Angeles Rams, a ceremony was held
at Green Bay's Brown Country Arena, adjacent to Lambeau
Field. Numerous celebrities and dignataries were on hand,
including President Nixon. Cherry was presented with a locket
that contained a microfiche telegram with over forty thousand signatures of Packer fans from all over the country. She
and I were equally moved by a gesture from George Allen.
Coach Allen had the entire Los Angeles team attend. The
following afternoon they were in attendance again, played
exceptionally well, and spoiled a special occasion for me.
Coach Allen doesn't forget either. Unfortunately, the fans
had a lot more to boo about. We struggled through the season,
finishing with a disappointing 6-8 record. Shortly after our
final game, Coach Bengtson announced his resignation.

Bengtson's role as a succesor to Lombardi was not an
enviable one. He inherited a team that was starting to experience the deterioration of its strength, and yet he was
expected to produce an NFL championship each year. Bengtson, an excellent defensive coach, had been a Packer assistant for all of the nine years Lombardi was head coach. His
coaching style reflected his reserved personality. This was a
sharp contrast to Lombardi. Perhaps the factor that was most
limiting to his success was one over which he had virtually
no control. He coached in the wake of one of the greatest
coaches in the history of football. And his ability was meas-
ured by the standard of excellence set by Lombardi.

Bengtson's successor was Dan Devine, a highly successful
college coach at Missouri and Arizona State. Despite an ailing shoulder, I decided to forgo retirement and help the
Packers through the transition, as I had under Bengtson.

The problems I was experiencing with my shoulder
prompted the team's physicians to recommend a specialized
examination at the Mayo Clinic in Rochester, Minnesota. The

examining physician, Dr. Ed Henderson, diagnosed a damaged tendon. He was confident that he could alleviate the problem by removing the damaged portion. The process would involve cutting a keyhole-shaped opening in the bone of my upper arm, severing the tendon, knotting it, and then inserting the knot into the hole.

I was very hesitant about undergoing surgery at that stage of my career and initially decided against it. But as training camp approached, the soreness got worse and I returned to the Mayo Clinic for the operation.

The surgery seemed to go off without a hitch, and Dr. Henderson was pleased, so I returned home to recuperate. But three days later my bandages were still soaked with blood. It did not cause me any immediate concern, as the doctor had explained that some bleeding would occur.

The next morning Cherry said to me, "Honey, you look awfully pale."

Despite a feeling of weakness, I said, "I'll be fine, dear."

"But look at those bandages, Bart. The bleeding hasn't stopped. It's worse. I'm calling Dr. Brusky."

Dr. Eugene Brusky, the Packers' team physician, took one look at my arm and immediately called the Mayo Clinic. While his assistant was arranging a chartered flight to Rochester, he said, "Bart, you need emergency treatment. The bleeding has broken your sutures."

Two hours later we landed in Rochester, and I was in danger of bleeding to death. I was rushed from the airport to the Mayo Clinic, where Dr. Henderson examined me. He was furious. He discovered that his assistant had failed to close off a small artery during the final stages of the operation. I had been bleeding from the artery for nearly a week.

I was unable to return until the end of the season and performed poorly when I did. There had been some nerve damage as a result of the operation and I had problems gripping the football. A thin leather glove that I had specially designed helped some but I could not throw the ball effectively.

My final appearance as a Green Bay Packer occurred against Miami, in the last game of a miserable 4-8-2 season. The

Dolphins had an excellent team and were on their way to Super Bowl VI. Coach Devine started me in the game despite the problems I was experiencing. In the third quarter, after throwing a pass that hit the ground 5 yards in front of the intended receiver, I ran to the sideline and said, "Coach, we'd be better off with Scott [Hunter]." Devine, however, did not replace me, and I continued to struggle the rest of the game. We were defeated easily, 27–6.

Despite my frustrating performance, I still did not want to retire and dedicated myself thoroughly to a rigorous rehabilitation program under the supervision of Dominic Gentile, the Packers' outstanding trainer. We both worked extremely hard during the entire off-season, and the chronic soreness in the front of my shoulder faded. I continued to experience severe pain while throwing, however, and realized that I could be only a shadow of the quarterback I once had been.

I officially announced my retirement shortly after the beginning of training camp in '72. Coach Devine asked me to stay on as a full-time member of his staff and work with the quarterbacks. Although I had not contemplated a coaching career, I accepted his offer with the understanding that I would remain for the '72 season only.

It turned out to be a very rewarding experience. The Packers had a pair of young quarterbacks, Scott Hunter and Jerry Tagge, whom I enjoyed working with. In addition, the Packers regained the Central Division title before losing to Washington, 16–3, in the playoffs.

Coach Devine was great to work for and extended numerous courtesies to Cherry and me during and after the season.

The only disagreement I ever had with him occurred during that loss to Washington, when I fought to permit Hunter to pass more versus a five-man line, which the Skins played to shut down our strong running game.

Green Bay remained our home as I traveled to Birmingham frequently to further establish Bart Starr Motor Co., the automobile dealership I co-owned. I also traveled often on speaking engagements and in my work as a television analyst for CBS Sports. I enjoyed telecasting as it kept me in touch with football.

In Green Bay, the excitement over the 1972 season quickly faded as the Packers suffered two straight losing seasons. In December 1974, Dan Devine resigned.

# CHAPTER

## 13

The most difficult decision of my life was not made on a football field or during the course of a meeting. It was made in the bedroom of my home in De Pere, Wisconsin. For the second consecutive night, I could not sleep as I weighed the pros and cons of accepting the job every Packer fan talks about.

Following the 1974 football season, I was offered a three-year contract to become Green Bay's head coach and general manager. The case against taking the job was strong. Lombardi's own words were a warning: "In pro football today, it's almost impossible to be both coach and general manager if you want to do well at either."

To a man, my close friends urged me not to. Bob Skoronski, the offensive captain of the Packers during most of my career as a player, was particularly adamant. "Bart," he said, "you have nothing to gain. Also, you're not prepared for the job . . . you don't have the experience."

He was right. I had only one year of coaching experience—in 1972, when I was the quarterback coach for Dan Devine.

Bob also pointed out that my business interests were promising enough that there was no need to become involved in such a risky undertaking.

The most compelling rationale for turning down the position had nothing to do with my qualifications or concern over job security, however. The Green Bay Packer organization had deteriorated to the point where it was one of the worst in pro football. Yet I was intrigued by the challenge of fielding an NFL team as well as rebuilding the Packers to the point where they would be as respected as they had been during the Lombardi era. The decision was made.

On December 24, 1974, I accepted the Packers' offer, despite all that sound advice to the contrary. What I lacked in experience would be made up through hard work and enthusiasm. "I ask for your prayers and your patience; we will earn everything else," I told the people of Wisconsin. How naïve. Little did I know how hard we would have to work to earn anything.

I thought that my first order of business would be to quickly assemble a coaching staff. For some reason, however, the Packer organization failed to release Devine's assistant coaches following his resignation. That unpleasant task was left for me.

Dave Hanner, who had been Devine's defensive coordinator, agreed to stay on with me. He was the first assistant I appointed and the only coach I retained from the previous staff. Burt Gustafson, Devine's linebacker coach, returned two years later to coach our special teams, however.

In hindsight, I erred in not offering positions to Rollie Dotsch and Red Cochran. Following a two-year stint at Detroit, Rollie was hired by Chuck Noll and was instrumental in Pittsburgh's success during their Super Bowl years. Red Cochran was an excellent offensive backfield coach with a tremendous amount of experience, and I could have learned a great deal from him.

An encounter while broadcasting a Lions-Vikings game during the '74 season led to the hiring of my first assistant coach after Dave. Ed Khayat, a Detroit assistant coach, told me, "Bart, if you ever get back into coaching and need a linebacker coach, that's your man right there." He was pointing to John Meyer.

I learned that assembling a quality coaching staff was as difficult as acquiring top-flight players. New England's Red Miller had been a highly respected assistant coach for fifteen years. I recognized the importance of hiring coaches with extensive experience in order to compensate for my lack thereof, and desperately wanted Red to join my staff. I thought he would until we ran into a major problem. The Green Bay Packers were the only team in the league that did not participate in the NFL coaches' pension plan. Although the Packers had their own separate plan, a coach did not receive credit for the years he had spent with other teams in determining when, or to what degree, he was vested. The NFL plan, on the other hand, used total years of service regardless of the team an individual coached for, as long as the team was a participant in the plan. I couldn't fault Red for turning down the offer. The retirement-plan situation cost us dearly. Two years later, Red took over as head coach of the Broncos and led them to the Super Bowl. The Packers finally joined the retirement plan that same year.

I hired Paul Roach as our offensive coordinator. Paul came to Green Bay from the Raiders with a strong background in offensive strategy. I felt extremely fortunate to get someone of his caliber. I also managed to hire one of the finest assistant coaches in the game, Lew Carpenter. Lew, a coach who excels in both the classroom and evaluation of personnel, helped develop Ken Burrough into an explosive deep threat at Houston. My old buddy Zeke Bratkowski came from Chicago to help develop our quarterbacks. Zeke was an outstanding teacher who made an immediate impact in this critical area.

Over the years I had the opportunity to assemble a coaching staff that I was proud of. Aside from John Meyer, Bill

Curry, Ernie McMillan, Zeke Bratkowski, and Lew Carpenter, several other men had outstanding careers at Green Bay. The first is Bob Schnelker, who possesses one of the finest minds in the game and is an outstanding game-day coach. Dick Rehbein, who started with the Packers as an obscure training-camp player, eventually became an outstanding special-teams coach. John Brunner deserves special mention as a supurb coach, especially while working with the running backs. Secondary coach Dick Lebeau, now the defensive coordinator of the Cincinnati Bengals was terrific. Bill Meyers, a bright young offensive line coach, contributed for two years.

Right away we began to evaluate the Packers' existing personnel and became very concerned. We simply did not have many talented players. Worse, we had inherited an aging football team. Nine players were over thirty, four more twenty-nine. The reasons for the Packers' decline after 1968 became more obvious; the organization had failed to adequately plan for the replacement of its quality veteran players. The coaches who succeeded Lombardi from 1968 were certainly not entirely responsible for such failure. In fact, the problems began in Lombardi's final years as head coach.

In 1974, during his last season as head coach, Dan Devine compounded the Packers' problems and severely limited the pace at which we could rebuild the team. Having given up Scott Hunter and Jerry Tagge, and desperate for a proven quarterback, Devine made a trade with the Rams for John Hadl. John was a superb athlete at the University of Kansas when Devine was coaching archrival Missouri. Although he had an excellent season at Los Angeles in 1973, Hadl was slipping noticeably in 1974. The price paid for him was mind-boggling.

When Hadl arrived in midseason, Fred Carr saw him enter the Packers' locker room and asked Jim Carter, his teammate at linebacker, "What did we give up for him?"

Carter paused and delivered his response in the best tradition of Lawrence Welk: "A one, a two, and a one, two, three." Carter's unique description of the compensation the Packers gave to the Rams was both humorous and accurate;

Green Bay gave Los Angeles its first- and second-round draft choices in 1975 and its first, second, and third in 1976.

Now, as we hustled to prepare for the January college draft, I realized that the Packers' inability to consistently procure quality pleayers was largely attributable to the inefficiency of their college scouting operation. It was antiquated. Not only were reports on prospective players not computerized, they were unorganized. The scouting department was also grossly understaffed. Lloyd Eaton, formerly a highly successful head coach at the University of Wyoming, was the Packers' director of player personnel. To his credit, he worked hard and did the best he could with the resources available. On draft day, I quickly learned how limited they were.

Our first two picks, Bill Bain in the second round and Willard Harrell in the third, were good choices. In the fourth, we drafted a classy overachiever from Ohio State named Steve Luke. Once again, we had done pretty well, but we could have had a steal. Our Big 10 scout was a retired high school coach who only worked part-time. When our turn came up, I looked at our talent board and said, "What can you tell me about Rick Upchurch of Minnesota?" He had almost no information. But the Denver Broncos, picking after us, knew something about him, and were rewarded with electrifying kick returns for nine years.

Our first training camp was six months away, but, in one respect, I wish it had been six years. There were no successful head coaches in the National Football League who had not first served an extended apprenticeship under professional or collegiate coaches. The decision of the Packer executive committee to appoint me as coach and general manager was based on emotion rather than logic. Perhaps they were attempting to maintain a link with the Lombardi era. I was not the best man for the job, but I accepted and promised them my best effort. I needed a crash course.

At the NFL league meetings that March in Hawaii, I cornered other coaches for advice. I was not concerned with game strategy, as I was already knowledgeable in that facet of the game, but organization and philosophy. Each of the most successful coaches I visited with was extremely helpful. Cherry and I went to dinner with Don and Dorothy Shula, and our wives must have thought I was a detective drilling a suspect . . . Don hardly had time to eat his dinner.

Later that spring, I flew to Columbus, Ohio, to spend some time with Woody Hayes. I looked forward to learning some of the practical aspects of running a football team and dealing with players, but I never dreamed I would learn so much in five minutes. I was observing the Ohio State spring practice drills while standing on the sidelines with Lou Holtz, the head coach at North Carolina State and a former Hayes assistant. Woody called me to the center of the field and asked me to say a few words to his Buckeye team.

As I stepped in front of the players, I felt a sudden jerk on the back of my collar. Hayes literally yanked me away, pushed me aside, and said, "Damn you! Don't you know that a good field general doesn't address his troops when they have to look into the sun?"

Most of the coaches and general managers I had yet to approach took the initiative to contact me, and not necessarily to wish me good luck. Sid Gillman, the general manager of Houston, realized that I would be looking to upgrade the level of athletic ability on our team and called to offer his castoffs. Gillman, long one of the most venerable and ingenious coaches in the league, was particularly insistent about taking advantage of the new kid on the block.

After taking his call for about the fourth time, and hearing him try to convince me to trade for his worst players, I finally had enough. "Coach," I said bluntly, "I have known you a long time, we're friends, and I have a tremendous amount of respect for you, but this is insulting."

The one call I'm glad I never received regarding a trade was from Don Shula. In 1973, he managed to convince the Packers that an inconsistent left-handed quarterback named Jim Del Gaizo was worth two second-round draft choices. Del Gaizo was gone before I took over, and I knew then I had better watch myself before talking too seriously with Don.

Had Don or Sid offered one of their quality veterans, I would have listened attentively. We simply did not have much returning talent. The team's best player the previous year, linebacker Ted Hendricks, refused to return, so I traded him to the Oakland Raiders for a pair of number-one picks. Our best performers were cornerback Willie Buchanon, linebackers Fred Carr and Jim Carter, and tight end Rich McGeorge. Gale Gillingham, the only remaining player from the Lombardi era, was so discouraged by the Packers' prospects that he took a one-year sabbatical. He returned the following season and then retired. Fortunately, our offensive line had a quality center in the best tradition of the Packers, Larry McCarren.

Our most glaring weakness was the offensive backfield. Hadl had seen his best years at quarterback. Although he was a great competitor and an inspirational leader, his arm was beginning to tire. I was sorry that I wasn't coaching him in his prime.

The running-back situation was not much better. John Brockington, a product of the Woody Hayes machine at Ohio State, burst into the league in 1971 and set it on fire. He rushed for more than 1,000 yards in each of his first three years in the league, and gained over 800 in 1974. Brock's production fell rapidly, however, and he only gained 434 yards in my first year. Two years later, when he should have been in his prime at age twenty-eight, we released him. His fall from greatness was a complete mystery.

Brock's backup at fullback, Barty Smith, was a bruising number-one pick from Virginia in 1973. His failure to develop into a premier running back was not a mystery at all —he suffered a serious knee injury in his rookie year that restricted his mobility, then he went down again with a bad knee in 1976. His misfortune was a real shame, because he left nothing on the field and would have killed to play on a winning team.

We did have an unexpected bright spot in training camp, one that took me back fifteen years. In 1960 Willie Wood had asked for and received a tryout with the Packers. Although no one gave him much of a chance, his attitude and aggressiveness caught everyone's attention within a few days. In my first training camp as a coach, another free agent safety from California (Cal State Fullerton), Johnnie Gray, laced up his shoes, slipped on number 24 (Willie's old number), and knocked our socks off. He started every game that season and quickly became known, along with fellow rookie Steve Luke, as one of the "Hit Brothers."

As we approached our first preseason game, a contest at Lambeau Field against the Buffalo Bills, we were short on talent but long on courage. Unfortunately, the fans and the media got the wrong impression. Willard Harrell, our rookie running back from Pacific, fielded a punt and raced about 70 yards for a touchdown. We went on to beat Buffalo in a meaningless game, but you would have thought we had won our division. Sports Illustrated immediately ran a feature article on my decision to take over the Packers job. Their brilliant photographers captured my excitement on Willard's punt return and placed the picture on their cover, along with the caption DREAMS OF GLORY IN GREEN BAY. It was nice to see our team on the front of the nation's leading sports publication, but I couldn't believe that they didn't realize we were actually many years away from fielding a successful football team.

The Packer fans who thought we might surprise some people were quickly brought down to earth. It took one play for them to realize that luck was not going to be an ally in 1975. Our kicker, Chester Marcol, who coming off another banner season and had established himself as one of the premier kickers in the league, tore the quadricep muscle in his right leg on the opening kickoff of our first regular-season game. He missed the rest of the season and never completely recovered. During the same game, we had two punts blocked and eventually succumbed to the Lions, 30–16.

Our special-teams coach, Bob Lord, had to fly home because of a family emergency before our next game, a Monday-night affair in Denver. Linebacking coach John Meyer and I literally revamped our punt-protection scheme and implemented it the day before the game. We didn't have any more punts blocked but also didn't have the horses to win the game.

Later that week, Bart junior and some of his friends, most of whom were not yet eighteen, decided to sneak into a local strip joint to see the eighth and nineth wonders of the world. Chesty Morgan had brought her sixty-inch boobs to Green Bay and the kids weren't about to miss them. Bart and his buddies pulled up some chairs right in front of the stage and ordered a few beers. As they waited for Chesty to make her appearance, Bart noticed one of our guards, Bruce Van Dyke, sitting across the stage. Bruce was a quick-witted individual, never at a loss for words, and that night was no exception. He hopped up from his chair, walked over to Bart, and said, "I won't tell if you won't." They both burst out laughing, and Bruce kept his word.

We needed all the light moments we could get as we dropped two more games to go 0-4. Our next opponent, the Dallas Cowboys, had a record of 4-0 and were on their way to Super Bowl X. Because of the unique hole in the roof of Cowboy Stadium and the forecast of clear skies, I decided to hold a special practice on Saturday in Dallas.

The purpose was to allow our players to acclimate themselves to the stadium and allow our punt returners to track the flight of a punt through varying backgrounds. Depending on the time of day, the ball could start off in the shadows, move directly into the sunlight, then back into shadows.

In the actual game we played as hard as we could for about fifty-seven minutes, but still trailed 17–12, and had to punt. David Beverly booted the ball into the sun. As it approached the Cowboys' punt returner, it disappeared into the shadows and went through his hands. We recovered, scored the game-winning touchdown, and celebrated our first victory.

We won only three of the remaining nine games, but we were never outhustled. Our 4-10 record was shameful, but our effort was Grade A. All we lacked was about ten or fifteen quality football players.

# CHAPTER

## 14

As I flew to Mobile in January 1976 to watch the Senior Bowl, I knew we needed to improve our quarterback situation if we were ever going to be competitive. The top-ranked quarterback in the draft, Richard Todd of Alabama, would be long gone before we had a chance to draft him. It was becoming more and more apparent that the only way we could upgrade ourselves in this critical position was through a trade. The man I wanted was Lynn Dickey of the Houston Oilers.

Lynn had had a brilliant career at Kansas State University, and was drafted by the Oilers in the third round in 1971. Five other outstanding collegiate quarterbacks—Jim Plunkett, Archie Manning, Dan Pastorini, Ken Anderson, and Joe Theismann—were drafted that year. Pastorini, in fact, was the Oilers' first-round selection, and either he or Lynn was going to be relegated to reserve duty.

For a while, it looked like Pastorini would be sitting on

the bench, as Dickey was playing exceedingly well. In 1972, however, Lynn severely dislocated his hip, had to practically learn how to walk all over again, and lost his starting job. Now, after five years of inactivity, it was time for him to play.

Bum Phillips, the head coach of the Oilers, and I sat down to discuss my desire to trade for Lynn. I told him candidly why I needed Dickey, and what I was willing to give up. He discussed what he was looking for, and we agreed that I would give him John Hadl, defensive back Ken Ellis, and two draft choices (a number 3 and number 4) for our new quarterback. The trade was good for both teams.

In order to protect our investment, we drafted a big offensive tackle from Colorado named Mark Koncar with one of the first-round picks we had received from Oakland in the Ted Hendricks trade.

I hardly had a good record when it came to personnel decisions, however. In my first year, I traded MacArthur Lane, a halfback, to Kansas City for a draft choice. Some members of the Packer staff feared that he was too outspoken and posed a disruptive threat to the team. On the other hand, I liked Mac very much personally and thought he might provide good leadership for our younger players. I should have overruled them and kept him, but I deferred to their judgment. Mac went on to play very well for the Chiefs; I kicked myself for letting him get away.

In 1976 I was faced with another gut-wrenching decision. When Chester Marcol had injured his leg the previous season, we picked up a free-agent kicker named Joe Danelo to take his place. Joe kicked very well for us and with his enthusiasm quickly endeared himself to his teammates. He was an excellent competitor who wasn't hesitant to get angry when he kicked poorly, yet he never became overemotional or depressed.

As we approached our final cutdown date, I had to decide whether to keep Chester or Joe. Chester had recovered from his injury physically. Psychologically, I couldn't tell. He seemed to be a little hesitant to really cut loose and hit the ball, and I couldn't blame him. In the back of my mind, I

thought he might return to the form he showed earlier in his
career, when he was one of the best the NFL had to offer.
Like the Packers' decision to hire me, my decision to keep
Chester was an emotional one. And like MacArthur Lane,
Joe went to his new team (the Giants) and played very well.
Chester struggled and never did regain his touch.

Although we were able to win three consecutive games
in midseason, our 1976 record, 5-9, was only a slight improvement from the year before. After the season was over,
I was forced to make a move that made the Lane and Danelo
trades look like a piece of cake.

Unlike the players I inherited, the coaches who joined
me in 1975 were taking a tremendous risk. They had no
pension plan to rely on, no winning organization to fit within.
Paul Roach, who helped run our offense, left a Raider team
that won the Super Bowl while we finished 5-9. Despite the
strong personal feelings I had for Paul, however, I was preparing to let him go.

Paul brought the Raiders' offensive philosophy to us and
knew every last detail. Oakland played fundamental, straight-
ahead football and simply overpowered people while keeping their mistakes to a minimum. They had the players to
pull it off. We did not.

Because of this lack of talent, we could move the ball
only if we were willing to resort to unusual formations and
deceptive plays, gimmicks. Practically every expansion team,
starting with the Dallas Cowboys in 1960, resorted to such
deception to cover weaknesses in personnel. We were no
better than most expansion teams and worse than some. Paul,
however, believed we would be better off sticking to a conservative approach. Zeke Bratkowski and I were equally strong
in our convictions that we needed to experiment. Turmoil
within our staff began to grow until I decided to end it. I
thanked him for his efforts and wished him well. Paul, to
his credit, took the news like a pro and moved on. In ret-
rospect, it was a move that would ultimately help everyone
involved.

For the first time since I had arrived, we had the opportunity, in early 1977, to really help ourselves in the draft. Our scouting system was dramatically improved, as we added qualified individuals to join perceptive scouts like Lloyd Eaton and Red Cochran. Equally important, we finally had our own first-round pick, plus the second first-round choice obtained in the Hendricks draft. Our top priority was to find some players who could rush the passer. Clarence Williams and Alden Roche, our incumbent defensive ends, were fierce competitors, but they were also aging and possessed only marginal quickness.

With the first of our two first-round selections, we chose Mike Butler, a tall, strong defensive end from Kansas. Our decision to select him came as no surprise, since he was regarded as one of the top defensive linemen in the draft. Our next pick, however, had everyone scratching their heads.

A few weeks earlier, Dick Corrick, our director of pro personnel, flew to Atlanta to work out a defensive end named Ezra Johnson. Our coaches and scouts had reviewed a considerable amount of film on Ezra, including a post-season game, and we were highly impressed. He was the furthest thing from a polished player—in fact, he didn't have the foggiest idea how to properly get down in a three-point stance. As a stand-up defensive end at Morris Brown University, he never needed to. At six-four, 240 pounds, and lean, he was a remarkable physical specimen. Dick called me after running Ezra through a series of drills and said, "Bart, he's a real find."

Dick was right on the money in more ways than one. Physically, Ezra was even more impressive than we thought. When we later timed him in the 40-yard dash, I looked at my watch and it read 4:49, or a shade under four and a half seconds. I assumed my clocking was off a little, and it was, but not the way I had anticipated . . . I had the slowest reading of the three coaches who were timing him. Besides his physical attributes, the quality Ezra possessed that made me decide to draft him was his work ethic. He could have been excused for going less than all out, because his ability would have carried him a long way. But Ezra worked just as hard as those less gifted, and we knew we had a gem when we drafted him.

But we were not the only ones who knew that. A minute after we announced our pick, I received a phone call from George Allen, the coach of the Washington Redskins.

"Bart," he said, "why did you take that guy so early?"

"We didn't think he would last very long," I replied.

"Well, I think it was a bit early but he can play. Good luck."

George was correct. We did select Ezra early, and he could play. Ezra quickly became one of the league's most feared pass rushers.

We had a whale of a draft in 1977, picking ten players who made our squad, including offensive tackle Greg Koch, running back Terdell Middleton, guard Derrel Gofourth, and quarterback David Whitehurst. As is usually the case, though, only a few of them made major contributions during their rookie seasons, and it took them awhile to get used to playing at the professional level.

They received an inexcusably rude indoctrination during the preseason. In August we hosted a strong New England Patriots team in Milwaukee, and we got killed. They ran over us, around us, and through us. They also made the mistake of rubbing our nose in the dirt.

In the fourth quarter, we were trailing by about twenty-five or thirty points and doing nothing offensively. We were playing reserves at every position and had barely put in our blitz-pickup blocking scheme. None of those factors deterred the Patriots from blitzing us on practically every play, often with first-stringers. The National Football League coaches generally adhere to an unwritten rule that says, "Thou shalt not intentionally humiliate an opponent once the game has been clearly decided." Chuck Fairbanks, the Patriots' coach, apparently chose to ignore it.

Once the game ended, I ran across the field to confront Chuck.

"I'm going to shake your hand," I said. "But I think you're

a first-class jerk. I don't know when, but I'm going to get your ass for this."

The 1977 season was a paradox. Our record was embarrassing at 4-10. We failed to move the ball effectively through the air or on the ground, primarily because, with the exception of quarterback, we lacked big-play men on offense. And in week nine, we lost our best offensive player because of a decision I made that I'll always deeply regret.

Late in the game against the Los Angeles Rams, I decided to let Lynn continue quarterbacking our offense, even though we were far behind. Under normal circumstances, I would have removed him, but Lynn was finally beginning to throw the ball well after struggling earlier in the game, and I thought he needed to regain his confidence. Then tragedy struck. Lynn dropped back to pass, and, as he planted his left leg, he suddenly collapsed. Larry Brooks, the Rams' defensive tackle, had literally crawled under his blocker, then dived directly into Lynn's leg, shattering the tibia and fibula. His leg was gruesome-looking and he was in excruciating pain as I accompanied him to the ambulance. I felt overwhelming guilt. Lynn had battled back from his hip surgery in Houston, a dislocated shoulder in our previous year, and now was in agony as a result of my decision.

I asked Dr. Brusky for an assessment.

"Bart, this one is really bad. He might be able to play again, but I can't tell you when." Lynn missed two years as a result of the injury.

Had the Packers decided to release me after the 1977 season, I wouldn't have blamed them. Our record on the field was the same as it had been in my first year at the helm. The aura of the Lombardi years sustained me, however, and I was given an extension.

Despite our record, we were making tremendous progress. In 1977, the Packers received two new additions to the coaching staff to work with our offensive linemen. Bill Curry, a long-time friend and former teammate, was responsible for the dramatic improvement in our offensive line. One of the classiest men you will ever meet, he is now the head coach at the University of Alabama. Bill and I then recruited Ernie McMillan to be his assistant. Ernie worked extremely well in that capacity and assumed control of our offensive line when Bill left a few years later. Ernie was one of the most knowledgeable, hardworking, and dedicated coaches I had the pleasure of working with.

Aside from the enlargement of our coaching staff, our facilities had been upgraded, including a first-class weight room. Our off-season conditioning program was dramatically improved and strides were being made in several other vital areas. The 1978 draft would be crucial to the Packers' long-term success.

# CHAPTER

## 15

I awoke on the morning of the 1978 draft thinking about the
Buffalo Bills. Chuck Knox was taking control of an organization that had fallen on hard times since the departure of
the Juice, O. J. Simpson. They would be picking fifth in the
draft, one spot ahead of us.

Houston, drafting first with a pick obtained from Tampa
Bay, chose running back Earl Campbell of Texas. Kansas City
followed by selecting Art Still, a defensive end from Kentucky. New Orleans, drafting third, took Florida receiver Wes
Chandler, followed by the New York Jets, who shored up
their offensive line by picking Ohio State tackle Chris Ward.

Buffalo was up next. They needed a game breaker as badly
as we did, but we coveted a receiver and hoped they would
choose Terry Miller, a quick running back from Oklahoma
State. As I waited for their selection, I thought to myself,
"Buffalo, don't take Lofton."

Pete Rozelle stepped up to the microphone and announced, "The Buffalo Bills take . . . running back Terry Miller. . . ." We quickly followed by drafting James Lofton, a wide receiver from Stanford University, and we knew this would help the team move the football.

James was primarily a track star at Stanford, running sprints and relays and winning national long-jump contests. However, during his senior year at Stanford, he blossomed as a receiver and terrorized the Pac-10 with his speed, moves, and cunning. Once we picked him, we were able to turn our attention to defense.

Our second choice in the first round was used to select John Anderson, a linebacker from Michigan who, at six feet three and 209 pounds, was considered "too light" by many scouts. Our scouting department was now first-rate, and believed he was capable of putting on a substantial amount of weight. He checked into our camp at about 222. If we had done nothing else during the draft, we wouldn't have been embarrassed, because we knew that Lofton and Anderson would step right in and help us. We were just warming up, though.

Eight draft choices in all, including linebackers Michael Hunt and Mike Douglass, defensive back Estus Hood, guard Leotis Harris, and defensive lineman Terry Jones, made the team. We were rebuilding.

With the infusion of new talent and a hunger for winning that bordered on starvation, we roared out of the block, winning six of our first seven games. Our fourth game of the year, played in the midst of the Santa Ana winds in San Diego, was typical of the effort we put forth. We really had no business whipping San Diego, as they were a far superior team. But at halftime I realized that the game would be won by the team that could best play in the heat. I challenged our players: "I know we are in better physical condition than those guys. To win this game, you're going to have to be mentally tougher as well. Someone is going to collapse out there, and it won't be us." San Diego turned the ball over eleven times as we won handily, 24–3. Tommy Prothro, the Chargers' head coach, was released the following week and replaced by Don Coryell.

On October 15, in Game 7, we hosted the Seattle Sea-hawks and made a little boy's dream come true. Steve Odom, our return specialist heard about a young child who was dying of cancer in Milwaukee. Steve promised him that he would run back a kick for a touchdown. On the game's open-ing kickoff, Steve fielded the ball at our 5-yard line, weaved through the Seattle defenders, and sprinted 95 yards for a touchdown. We defeated the Seahawks, 45–28.

But as quickly as we ascended to the top of our division, we tumbled. Whereas earlier we had won handily, we now lost in devastating fashion. Against the Eagles in Philadel-phia, we ran up and down the field all day, only to fall prey to them 10–3 as a result of too many turnovers of our own.

Six weeks later, we hosted the Vikings, knowing that a victory would probably send us to the playoffs. We played our hearts out, and, with less than two minutes remaining, led 10–3. The Vikings were backed into their own territory, with no timeouts. The odds looked to be in our favor, but Fran Tarkenton enjoyed overcoming the odds. He completed two passes on fourth down, and finally tied the game with six seconds remaining on a pass to Ahmad Rashad. We fin-ished in 10–10 deadlock and never fully recovered. Our 8-7-1 record tied us with Minnesota for the Central Division title, but they made the playoffs because they had beaten us in an earlier meeting that year.

Most of the state's sportswriters described our perform-ance in the second half of the season as a collapse, or at least a mystery. There was really nothing baffling about it.

To begin with, we were not a 6-1 team after seven games. Our record was 6-1, but we were only an average team, not a good one. In addition, we were not yet a mature ball club. In fact, many of the major contributors to our success were in their first or second year in the NFL. This factor worked against us once we became the hunted rather than the hunter. We played the second half of the season with little or no chance of sneaking up on opponents. Finally, although we received great effort from David Whitehurst at quarterback, he was simply not the caliber of player Lynn Dickey was. As a result, we were unable to get the ball in Lofton's hands as often as we should have, although James' peers recognized his contribution by voting him into the Pro Bowl as a rookie.

The bumper stickers reading THE PACK IS BACK were a few years premature.

We may have been disappointed over missing the play-offs, but we were definitely not discouraged. In fact, we were confident that another strong draft would put us over the hump. We got off to an excellent start by choosing a blue-chip running back, Eddie Lee Ivery of Georgia Tech, in the first round. Our decision was not a reflection of dissatisfaction with the play of Terdell Middleton, the incumbent halfback; he had rushed for over 1,000 yards the previous year and always played his heart out. Rather, we simply could not pass on a back as versatile and accomplished as Ivery. By adding another player with big-play capability, we would not only improve our rushing attack but also divert some of the opposing defense's attention away from Lofton. If Lynn Dickey could return, our offense had the potential to score from anywhere on the field.

I blew our next two picks.

In the second round, we chose another talented runner, Steve Atkins of Maryland. He had as much natural ability as Ivery and was even bigger than Eddie Lee. Steve lasted until the second round, mostly because of an "undera-chiever" label. Although he worked hard for us and was easy to coach, the return on investment of this high choice never fully materialized.

The following round, we picked another player from Maryland—defensive tackle Charles Johnson. Prior to the draft, the Packer defensive coaches lobbied fiercely for him. At the risk of sounding arrogant, I was a good judge of talent. My most serious mistakes inevitably occurred when I failed to follow my convictions and deferred to someone with more experience. Although Charles was a good team player and dedicated worker, I blundered.

The player I wanted to pick was Joe Montana, the quar-terback from Notre Dame. He lasted until the third round because those who evaluated his potential believed he lacked arm strength and the ability to withstand the punishment he would face from NFL linemen. Indeed, he was rather frail looking as a senior for the Irish.

Zeke Bratkowski, my closest friend and an excellent quarterback groomer, was sent to California to work out Joe Montana. When Zeke returned with the workout film, I was estatic. Joe clearly had the athletic ability to be a successful quarterback, and he possessed a frame large enough to carry additional muscle without losing his agility. Above all, he was a winner. Although Devine had periodically benched him at Notre Dame, Joe had directed some remarkable comebacks for the Irish, most notably in the 1979 Cotton Bowl. In that game, he overcame a bout with hypothermia to rally his team from a 34–12 deficit against Houston to a 35–34 victory. He would have been an excellent leader for us. From the moment we passed on him and took Johnson instead, I realized I had made a poor choice.

Fortunately, we found a diamond in the rough during the 1979 draft. Alabama was the national champion the previous year, posting a record of 11-1 and defeating Penn State in the Sugar Bowl. Their team was loaded with talent, and much of the NFL's attention was centered on Barry Krause, one of Alabama's inside linebackers. The Tide's other inside linebacker, Rich Wingo, played rarely during his senior year while attempting to shake himself of the injury bug. He was undersize at six-one and 230 pounds, and his speed was marginal. His background, work habits, and tenacity were second to none. We picked him in the seventh round.

During training camp, my dad, who had become a regular spectator at our summer sessions, was ecstatic. He had always been an avid Alabama fan, and when he saw one of Bear Bryant's players running around our drills knocking everyone's head off, he was in heaven. He came up to me following one of the practices, in which Wingo had delivered a stunning blow to a running back. "Son," he said, "that boy's a real football player. Ol' Bear taught him well." I smiled and nodded; Rich was playing like a confident veteran.

Halfway through training camp, however, he injured his back and was unable to practice for three weeks. Our final cutdown date was fast approaching, and we had seen so little of him in game conditions that it was a risky decision to keep him, but I was determined to make a place for him on our roster.

I shared my thoughts with Cherry one evening. She was always interested in the progress of the team and players, visiting training camp daily. The day before the final squad reduction was announced, she saw Rich sitting alone on a golf cart, nursing his sore back. Rich was terribly discouraged. Cherry walked over, put her arm on his shoulder to comfort him, and asked, "Are you worried about making the team?"

He nodded. Cherry couldn't stand to see the concerned look on his face. "Don't be," she said, "you've already made it. Just get a good night's sleep." Rich smiled and listened to her say, "And don't you dare tell anyone about this." They both laughed.

We finished the preseason schedule with a level of optimism and confidence unlike any we had felt even during our hot streak the previous year. Eddie Lee Ivery was brilliant during this period as he provided a new spark to an already improving offense. Lynn Dickey was finally beginning to recover from his broken leg, and David Whitehurst, his backup, had worked hard to improve his passing. Our defense was small but mean. If we could score enough points, they were capable of keeping us close to most opponents. We had an excellent shot at another winning record, as long as we stayed healthy and were able to avoid exposing our lack of depth.

Our archrivals, the Chicago Bears, hosted us in Game 1. Bear-Packer games were traditionally low-scoring affairs, and we didn't expect this one to be any different. For the first time in five years, we finally had a running back, Ivery, who could have the same type of impact on a game as Chicago's superstar, Walter Payton.

Midway through the first quarter, Eddie Lee took a handoff, swept to his left, and put a move on a Bear defender that

left the Chicago player grasping air but left Eddie Lee clutch-
ing his left knee. He had not taken a blow to his leg; rather,
his foot simply caught on the Soldier Field Astroturf and
refused to give. He severed a ligament and missed the remainder of the season.

Nineteen seventy-nine was just not meant to be our year,
as we regressed to a 5-11 record. There were, however, some
noteworthy exceptions to an otherwise forgettable season.

On September 23 we traveled to Minnesota to take on
the Vikings. Rich Wingo was now starting in place of Michael
Hunt, our starting middle linebacker who had also gone down
with a knee injury. Rich stepped in and set an all-time Packer
record for unassisted tackles. He was on his way to receiving
all-rookie awards and compliments from John Madden, who
called him "the finest rookie middle linebacker I've ever
seen." Rich was on top of his game against Minnesota, roam-
ing from sideline to sideline to help thwart the Vikings'
offensive attack.

Unfortunately, we lost two defensive linemen during that
game and tried fruitlessly to cling to a 21–14 lead. After
Minnesota tied the score 21–21, we had possession of the
ball near our 25-yard line with more than a minute remaining. I decided to run out the clock and take our chances in
overtime rather than risk a turnover in regulation, although
it was a close call.

We lost the overtime toss and kicked off to the Vikings,
who returned the ball into our territory. A play or two later,
they threw a scoring pass to defeat us, 27–21. It was a crush-
ing defeat.

As we entered the visitors' locker room, James Lofton
exploded. He threw his helmet into his locker and vented
his frustrations by questioning my decision to run out the
clock in regulation.

"We weren't playing to win," he shouted. "We were just
playing not to lose."

As much as I respected James, I could not allow him to
second-guess any of the coaches, including me. "Knock it
off," I said. "You play, I'll coach."

Ironically, James' tirade was the beginning of a relationship between us that grew stronger each year. I disliked the manner in which he expressed his feelings, but I admired the fact that he detested losing.

Eight days after that heartbreaking defeat, we were scheduled to host our old friends the New England Patriots. New England was one of the most talented teams in the National Football League, and very few prognosticators gave us a chance. I understood why. We were devastated by injuries, and depressed by our near miss at Minnesota. The Packers were going to play their thousandth game in front of millions of viewers on ABC's *Monday Night Football*. Most viewers were expecting a blowout and Don Meredith had his vocal cords finely tuned before the first kickoff.

A number of our players and coaches, however, remembered the anger we felt when New England rubbed our faces in the dirt two years before in a preseason game. In addition, our players responded to a challenge I issued to them during the week. I told them that the entire country would discover how much pride we had. We had a ton.

After falling behind, 7–0, we rallied to smash the Patriots 27–14. We outhit, outhustled, outplayed, and outcoached them. Davie Simmons, a rookie linebacker from North Carolina State, literally crushed three or four New England players on kickoff coverage, and he had lots of practice that night. The first nationally televised night game from Lambeau Field was our brightest moment all year.

With the return of Lynn Dickey in late 1979, the rehabilitation of Eddie Lee Ivery's knee, and the surprise discovery of free-agent tight end Paul Coffman, we had an offensive football team that could provide some balance to the explosive talents of James Lofton. We needed to improve our defense, however, if we were going to become a consistently winning football team.

We had converted our defense from a 4-3 to a 3-4, meaning we would use only three down lineman and four linebackers. The key to a successful defensive line under that alignment is a quality nose tackle, one who can dominate the other team's center. As the 1980 draft approached, we had our man.

Bruce Clark of Penn State was one of the most outstanding defensive-line prospects to come out of college in years. Before the draft, I flew to State College, Pennsylvania, in a private plane, along with John Meyer, our new defensive coordinator, and Herb Tressler, our orthopedic surgeon, to see Bruce.

He was a typical student athlete under Joe Paterno. Bruce was personable, warm, intelligent, and a gentleman. Herb examined the knee he had injured during his senior year and pronounced him fit.

John and I were interested in learning whether he had any reservations about playing nose tackle. It is the most difficult defensive position on the team, but he said he was anxious to give it a try. We also wanted to know how he felt about playing in Green Bay, Wisconsin. He told us how much he enjoyed the smalltown atmosphere of State College, and that he didn't want to play in a large city. We explained that his field of study, hotel management, would probably not land him a job in Green Bay, and we all chuckled.

As we flew back to Green Bay, our number-one draft choice was set. Incredibly, we never even made it to first base in our negotiations with him.

Almost immediately after we announced our choice, Bruce changed his tune. He said he had no intention of ever playing nose tackle. John Meyer and I could not believe what we were hearing. He had told us just the opposite only a few weeks earlier.

Clark's agent was Richard Bennett, a skilled negotiator from Washington, D.C. Bob Harlan, who handled player contracts for the Packers, mailed Bennett an initial offer. Rather than proceeding to enter into good-faith bargaining, however, Bennett quickly signed Clark to a contract with Toronto of the Canadian Football League, and for an amount far less than what we were prepared to offer him. Why did Bennett advise him to sign with Toronto?

Bruce Clark was not the only number-one draft choice that year who was represented by Bennett. In fact at least three or four others were, too. Bob Harlan and I quickly realized that Bennett was using Bruce Clark's decision to play in the Canadian Football League as leverage against the teams that drafted the other players he represented. Bennett's tactic was successful—his clients all signed lucrative long-term contracts.

I did not feel, however, that Bennett's advice to Bruce was necessarily in *Bruce's* best interest. Toronto is a terrific city and I'm sure Bruce enjoyed himself there. He would have also enjoyed Green Bay and gained valuable NFL experience. As much as we respected Bennett as an agent, we knew he didn't give us a fair shot.

Some members of the local media, as is so often the case, came down hard on us without thinking or doing their homework. Had they done so, they would have realized we did everything we could when preparing to draft Bruce.

We were still able to acquire some help in the draft, including linebacker George Cumby, defensive back Mark Lee, and offensive linemen Syd Kitson and Karl Swanke.

Our 1980 season was a peculiar one. Our record—5-10-1—was virtually the same as our mark in 1979. Yet, until the tail end of the season, we played exciting, competitive football and, with a break or two, could have had a good record.

We managed to lose a game in Cleveland in the final seconds when defensive back Mark Lee slipped on a pass thrown by Browns quarterback Brian Sipe that was underthrown by 5 yards.

In Pittsburgh, we gave away nine points via errant snaps to our punter and lost, 22–20.

But for the most frustrating experience all year, nothing topped our 14–14 overtime tie in Tampa Bay. The game left a bitter pill in my mouth, for a number of reasons. First, we gained 569 yards and should have scored at least twice as many points as we did. Second, we played as hard as possible, and dominated the Buccaneers all day, yet had nothing to show for it. Finally, our kicker, Tom Birney, missed two easy field goals; had he made either, we would have won the game.

The year was not simply one of heartache, however. Our opening game of the season provided the Green Bay fans with an opportunity to witness one of the gutsiest performances I can recall. Less than four weeks earlier, our center, Larry McCarren, had undergone hernia surgery. Larry had a consecutive-game playing streak that was into triple digits, but the team doctors told him the record was in serious jeopardy. We knew how much the streak meant to Larry, and devised a plan for him to keep it alive. Larry would snap the ball for one play, then watch the rest of the game from the sidelines while his backup took over.

Larry wanted no part of our idea. After the first play, we sent in his replacement, but Larry motioned him off the field. He continued to play the entire game—against the Bears, no less—and helped lead our team to a 12–6 victory in overtime. Most fans that day remember Chester Marcol catching his own blocked field-goal attempt in midair and running in for the game-winning touchdown. But when I reflect on that Chicago game, I think of Larry. His streak finally ended on Thanksgiving day in Detroit, Michigan.

November was an important month for us in two respects. First, we picked up Jan Stenerud to handle the kicking. Jan is one of the finest individuals I have ever met, and his stability and work habits made everyone on our team a better player. Second, we learned to improvise. As we prepared to tangle with the San Francisco 49ers in Milwaukee, we had to deal with a small problem ... we were almost out of linebackers.

Defensive coordinator John Meyer devised a creative defensive scheme that used five linemen, five defensive backs, and only one linebacker. He was an outstanding defensive coach who took pride in his teaching and organizing, and I was anxious to see John's scheme work.

On the 49ers' first play, Earl Cooper took a handoff and ran about 40 yards. They then proceeded to jump out to a 13–0 lead. Incredibly, however, our defense tightened, and we rallied. We were missing so many defensive players we actually had to use James Lofton as a free safety for a few plays, but we managed to win, 23–16.

Because of our poor finish in 1980, the Packer executive committee voted to strip me of my title as general manager. I was extremely disappointed in their decision. The logical move, in my opinion, would have been to retain me as the general manager and select a new coach. Our progress in areas most influenced through the general manager's role had been significant, for we were now a solidly structured organization.

Rather than fill the new void with a qualified football executive like Jim Finks or George Young, the Packers did not select someone to fill that vital slot until 1987, when Tom Braatz, formerly of the Atlanta Falcons, was hired. As the head coach it was now imperative for me to draft a player who could make an immediate impact on our team, much the way Lofton did and Ivery would have had he not been cut down by injury. We simply could not afford another Bruce Clark fiasco.

# CHAPTER

## 16

I am fascinated by the unwillingness of coaches and scouts to step up to the table and accept responsibility for wasting a draft choice. There is no question that I made a terrible mistake in passing on Joe Montana in 1979. He could play, I knew it, and I blew it. But if our decision to take Charles Johnson that year was a mistake, our selection of Rich Campbell over Ronnie Lott in 1981 was a colossal blunder. Don't misinterpret that statement. Rich was and is a quality person and fierce competitor with a lot of pride. He possessed excellent size (six feet-four, 220 pounds) and had compiled some impressive statistics before injuring a knee his senior year. We needed a young quarterback to groom as the eventual replacement for Lynne Dickey, who was into his thirties and battered. Everyone in our organization who was specifically assigned to evaluate Campbell, including me, gave him marks ranging from good to great. However, I was very concerned with a flaw in his delivery, which was best described as "short-armed" and prevented him from throwing the ball very hard. When I reviewed the film of the workout we put him through, I was even more concerned.

Ronnie Lott, a safety from the University of Southern California, would have been an immediate starter and star for any team. He had it all—size, speed, smarts. He also had an agent who hinted in no uncertain terms that Ronnie was not thrilled with the idea of playing in Green Bay. Of course, those threats were a dime a dozen and, with the exception of Bruce Clark, they were inevitably bluffs.

I preferred Lott.

The St. Louis Cardinals, picking directly before us, should have eliminated our dilemma. They decided to choose Campbell, but, incredibly, couldn't reach him. Like many teams, the Cardinals had a policy of not drafting someone until they had spoken to him by phone. They did not have Campbell's correct phone number, and were forced to choose Alabama linebacker E. J. Junior instead.

It was our turn to choose. I swore after the mistake of passing on Montana that I would listen to my gut instincts. I guess I would have to listen another time, because we called Campbell. Unfortunately, we didn't have the Cardinals' telephone book.

After the draft, most sportswriters praised me for selecting him. They assumed, since I had just been relieved of my duties as general manager, that I would pick Lott, who would have an immediate positive impact on our team. My choice of Campbell, they went on to say, was an indication that I was more concerned about the future of the Packers than I was about my future. I did care about the well-being of the Packers, and I appreciated their comments. Neverless, I should have taken Lott, who in just one season turned around San Francisco's defense and helped lead them to the Super Bowl.

Our season began in Chicago almost exactly as it had two years earlier. For Eddie Lee Ivery, the similarities were too much to bear. Once again, he got off to a fast start, and once again he found himself planting his left foot to make a sharp cut. He was on the same part of the field and his knee blew

out once more, tearing a different ligament. We won the game
this time around, but not many others, as we came out of
the block 2-6. Morale was high, however, despite the rumors
that I was on my way out.

After Game 3, we traded three high draft choices to San
Diego for wide receiver John Jefferson. With a healthy Lynn
Dickey throwing to J.J., James Lofton, and Paul Coffman, it
was only a matter of time before we began clicking.

Sure enough, we won six of our last eight games and
came within an eyelash of winning the Central Division title;
our loss to the Jets on the final weekend kept us out.

We received contributions from the usual stars and also
from the most unlikely of heroes. Mark Murphy, a free-agent
safety, played a major role, although earlier in the season it
didn't appear as though he would have much support from
his teammates.

One of the rules most rookies follow is fairly simple; don't
do anything to make yourself too conspicuous, at least if you
plan on making friends with the veterans. Mark walked into
the locker room his first day in Green Bay with a shaved
head. It didn't take long for his teammates to crank up the
comments: "Well, isn't he something. I guess the rookie is
too cool to worry about looking like the rest of us." Mark
said nothing.

He had never shaved his head; rather, he had a rare dis-
ease that caused him to lose his body hair. The vets, of
course, were red in the face when they discovered what Mark
had overcome.

We persevered as a team, too, and made some stirring
comebacks, including one against the Lions in early December at Lambeau Field. After the game, I gathered the team
into a huddle at midfield. I asked them to take a few minutes
to shake hands with the greatest fans in the world. Our devoted followers stuck with me as a coach and stood behind
our players as we struggled for years. We were now competitive again and I wanted them to know how much we
appreciated their support. The players enjoyed themselves
after that game as much as the fans.

The cheering was just beginning. Nineteen eighty-two was going to be our year.

We had an uneventful training camp, although we did sign one player as a free agent who was determined to make a name for himself. Larry Pfohl had been a solid offensive tackle in the Canadian Football League for many years, but he was unable to crack our lineup. He was, however, quite perceptive and was able to parlay his remarkable physique into a successful career in professional wrestling as Lex Lugar.

Our team stumbled badly in the first half of Game 1, as we fell behind the Rams, 23–0. When we entered our locker room at halftime, I kicked everyone out except for the coaches and players. Usually I was calm in my approach, but not today.

"That was the most disgraceful effort I have ever seen," I hollered. "If you don't have any more pride than what's on display in the first half, then go take your showers now." We climbed all over Los Angeles in the second half and concluded the greatest rally in Packer history, winning 35–23.

A few days after the game, the National Football League Players Association voted to go on strike. I was sick. I understood that they felt strongly about certain issues, but we had our best team and I was afraid we were going to miss our opportunity to make the playoffs.

The strike was set to begin, ironically, after our Monday-night contest the following week against the Giants in the New Jersey Meadowlands. We must have enjoyed playing catch-up football, because we proceeded to fall behind 19–7 to Ray Perkins's team. With the ball on our 17-yard line, Lynn Dickey handed the ball to Jim Jensen. He swept left and handed it off to James Lofton, who glided gracefully in the other direction on a reverse. James cut upfield behind a good block from Lynn and streaked down the sideline for an 83-yard touchdown that stunned the Giants. We went on to defeat them, 27–19, despite having to sit through a thirty-minute delay when the stadium lights went out.

Following the game, I addressed the strike head on. I told the players, "You have to assume you'll be playing again soon, even though it doesn't look like you will. The team that stays in the best condition will be the one that gets off to a fast start when you return. We'll get information to the captains tomorrow regarding the availability of St. Norbert College's facilities for your use."

As the strike lengthened, Cherry and I were caught in the middle of the tension between the players and management. The players' wives were still as friendly as ever toward her, however, and while playing tennis with Barbara Jensen one day, the subject of the traditional Halloween party came up.

Each year, the players and their wives had a costume party, but they were undecided whether to do so again because of the strike. Barbara told Cherry that the couples had recently decided to go ahead with the party, in hopes that it would boost everyone's spirits. The bash would be held at Nicky's, a fashionable pub in west De Pere.

Cherry and I were eating dinner a few nights before the party, when she suddenly declared, "Bart, we're going to crash the Halloween party. Let's get some costumes."

Initially, I was hesitant, but the more I thought about it, the better I liked the idea.

Finally she talked me into it.

I dressed up as an old farmer, complete with overalls and a red plaid shirt. I wore a pig mask over my face, and pillows inside my shirt to make me appear pudgy.

She wore a long silver dress and artificial boobs even Chesty Morgan would have envied. Her mask was that of a hideous-looking old witch, complete with gray stringy hair and a pointed nose.

For the final touch, we practiced changing our voices. We were prepared to stump everyone.

We entered Nicky's carrying a Mexican casserole, as each couple was responsible for one dish. About half the players and their wives were there, which suited us fine, because we intended to stay only a few minutes and then let them have some fun.

No one could figure out who we were. Nicky's had a poster of all the Packers on the wall, and the couples used a process of elimination. Linebacker John Anderson's wife, Susan, came up to me, squeezed my arm, and said, "It sure isn't a linebacker."

Syd Kitson, a normally shy offensive guard, waltzed with Cherry and kissed her right on the mouth, ugly mask and all. Good thing for Cherry, because the three bees were just entering the bar. Paul Coffman, Greg Koch, and Larry McCarren dressed up as a trio of bumblebees. Paul, who always had a way with ladies, danced Cherry all around the floor, unaware of who she was, let alone her escort. When the music stopped, he held her at arm's length, leered at her figure, and said, in a voice loud enough to capture everyone's attention, "You have great-looking tits!"

We immediately pulled off our masks. The players and their wives almost died laughing, and Paul nearly fainted. They insisted we stay, and we did, for about an hour and a half. We had a blast, and it turned out to be a real morale booster.

When the strike was over and we rode the bus to Milwaukee for our first game back, Cherry and I were sitting in the front row as the players boarded. Paul Coffman got on, saw her, and blushed. Cherry said, "By the way, Paul, thanks for the compliment."

We picked right up where we left off, hammering the Vikings, 26–7. The veterans deserve the credit for the fast start we had. They were able to keep the team together during the strike and everyone stayed in good shape.

Although the strike was over, the Packer organization decided not to hold its Thanksgiving dinner for the team. The players did hold one on their own and invited Cherry and me as their guests. Despite an inexcusable tie with the Colts late in the aborted season, we made the playoffs and were pumped with excitement.

For the first time since the "Ice Bowl," Green Bay hosted a playoff game against the St. Louis Cardinals. We blew them out, 41–16, and traveled to Dallas.

Very few football pundits gave us much of a chance against the Cowboys, and even the few who did must have wondered what was going on in the second quarter, as we trailed, 20–7. We refused to fold, however, rallied to cut their lead to 30–26, and threatened to win the game before losing, 37–26. The Green Bay fans acted as though we had won the game; they were ecstatic when they greeted us on our arrival from Dallas.

The Packer president, Robert Parins, a former circuit-court judge, acted as though we hadn't won a game all year. I had to work to get a mere two-year extension from him. I came away with an uneasy feeling.

I spent much of the off-season reflecting on the progress of our team. We had come a long, long way from 1975.

Our offensive line was gradually improving each year, led by the consistent play of center Larry McCarren and tackle Greg Koch. Koch, our second-round pick in 1977 from Arkansas, was underrated by the national press but appreciated by our coaching staff. He often played through back spasms while never losing his effectiveness. His buddy Paul Coffman had established himself as one of the NFL's best tight ends, as much a result of his blocking as of his receiving skills.

Our receivers, Lofton and Jefferson, were each all-pros. I was becoming concerned about J.J.'s work habits; he was not in very good shape when he reported to camp in the summer of 1982. Lofton, on the other hand, was in exceptional condition. In fact, Lofton came to camp in better shape every year I coached. When fans and analysts observed James in action, they inevitably referred to him as one of the "best natural athletes" in the game. James certainly is a graceful, fluid athlete, strong and swift. But those adjectives hardly tell the story behind his success. How did he become the best receiver in football?

To begin with, he's brilliant. He majored in industrial engineering at Stanford, but I didn't realize how sharp he was until he arrived in Green Bay for a special session. He had missed our first minicamp because of the NCAA long-jump competition, but flew to Green Bay once it was over. I quickly ran through our offensive terminology and philosophy, then asked him if he had any questions.

"No," he answered casually. "It's rather elementary, isn't it?"

James also worked so diligently in the off-season that he finished first in every series of tests we put our receivers through. He will be able to play at least another four or five years at a Pro Bowl level.

J.J., one of the most unselfish superstars I've known, neglected his off-season conditioning, and has been out of football for two years.

Our quarterbacking situation was solid after Lynn Dickey was fully recovered. With Lynn directing us we were capable of scoring from literally anywhere on the field. No deficit was too big to overcome.

My concern as I pondered the 1983 draft was our defense. Mike Butler, our defensive left end, had played out his option and was rumored to be talking to the Tampa Bay Bandits of the USFL. If we signed him, I could try to shore up our defensive backfield, where we needed depth. If we were going to lose Butler, I would have to consider drafting a lineman such as Jim Jeffcoat of Arizona State. During numerous discussions with Judge Parins, he assured me we would sign Butler.

Tim Lewis, from the University of Pittsburgh and the best defensive back available, was chosen with our first pick. I told Judge Parins it was imperative that we re-sign Butler. He replied, "No sweat. We'll get it done."

"We" didn't get it done and opened the season without him. That was inexcusable, since the two sides were very close to an agreement. It would have been worth the extra money.

Our sixteen-game roller coaster was not the best Packer team I ever played for or coached, but it was by far the most exciting. Offensively, we were practically unstoppable. We added a powerful fullback, Jessie Clark, and a tenacious guard, Dave Dreschler, to our lineup via the draft. On the rare oc-

casions when we were unable to move the ball, another rookie,
punter Bucky Scribner, kept our opponents off balance with
his left-footed spirals. Jan Stenerud, our placekicker, was as
reliable as always, and broke the all-time NFL record for
career field goals. We scored 429 points in sixteen games.
Unfortunately, we gave up 430.

Our inability to stop opponents from scoring had nothing
to do with lack of effort; rather, we were simply forced to
play a second- or third-string defensive line the entire year.
Butler's absence meant we had to start his backup, Byron
Braggs, who was strong and fast but lacked motivation. Still,
we would have posted a winning record had we avoided a
crippling series of injuries.

The Houston Oilers hosted us in the first game of the
year. We won the battle, 41–38, but began to lose the war.
Nose tackle Terry Jones, one of our unsung heroes, tore his
Achilles tendon and missed the remainder of the season. His
backup, Richard Turner, went down with a serious knee
injury five weeks later and was also sidelined for all further
games. It quickly became apparent that we were going to
have substantial difficulty stopping anybody, as Houston
nearly ran the ball down our throats, despite the fact that
Earl Campbell was clearly past his prime. But we were up
to the task as Lynn Dickey, playing with a migraine headache, completed twenty-seven of thirty-one passes, including his first eighteen attempts, for 333 yards and five
touchdowns.

Our home opener was the following week against Pittsburgh. The Steelers took advantage of their strength, center
Mike Webster, by running the ball right at us play after play.
We were simply unable to stop them, despite a great effort
from our defensive players.

The following week, we reverted to our pattern established in week one; we edged the Rams, 27–24, on a last-
second field goal by Jan Stenerud, just as we had defeated
the Oilers in our opening game. Incredibly, we lost yet another key defensive player, linebacker Randy Scott.

Like Rich Wingo, Randy arrived from Alabama as an unsung, small middle linebacker nobody else seemed to care about. Also like Rich, Randy played for Bear Bryant and learned a thing or two about winning. A few years after Rich woke up the experts with his unbridled enthusiasm, Randy did the same thing for us. Ironically, Randy got his first chance to prove his worth as a result of an injury suffered by Rich. Now, two years later, Randy's torn knee ligament meant that Rich would have to fill in for him, even though Rich's back wasn't fully recovered from the two serious operations he had undergone. We had no choice but to play him.

Our scoring machine reached the zenith of effectiveness two weeks later at Lambeau Field against the Tampa Bay Buccaneers. We scored from every conceivable angle and opportunity, and led Tampa Bay at halftime, 49–7. That total tied a record for most points in the first half of a game.

The outburst created a dilemma. We were forced to alter our game plan in the second half and played very conservatively. There was no way we were going to pour it on after halftime. We also forgot to pour it on the following week and our record was even at 3-3.

Four years after our first Monday-night game in Lambeau Field, when we trounced New England, the ABC camera crews came rolling in again. This time, our opponent was even more formidable—we faced the Washington Redskins, the defending Super Bowl champions. Most teams that win the championship have a letdown the following season. Not Washington. In fact, from the way they manhandled most of their first six opponents, it appeared as though they had just missed winning the Super Bowl and were determined not to blow it this time around.

The Skins rolled into Lambeau Field as prohibitive favorites, and rightfully so. After seeing the films of our banged-up defensive unit, they probably thought they could score every time they had possession of the ball. We felt the same way about them. Washington's defensive line was solid against the run, but we believed our offensive linemen could pass-block them effectively enough for Lynn Dickey to find our receivers. Both teams were correct in their assessments.

The final score—Green Bay 48, Washington 47—was the highest point total ever recorded on *Monday Night Football*. The game was just as exciting as the numbers indicated, with each team finding creative ways to take the lead. In the last minute, Jan Stenerud made a field goal and Mark Moseley missed, sending the Packer faithful into a frenzy.

We quickly brought everyone back down to earth by losing a 20–17 overtime heartbreaker to Minnesota. We continued our erratic pattern throughout the season, falling into the depths of frustration on November 27 in Atlanta.

The Falcons were not contending for their divisional title, but they were coming off a high, having defeated San Francisco the previous week on a last-second alley-oop pass from Steve Bartkowski to Billy "White Shoes" Johnson.

We needed every game we could get, of course, and the contest quickly began to resemble the aerial circus we had participated in with the Redskins. Our offense, as usual, was relentless, and we posted forty-one points. Our crippled defense, as usual, was vulnerable; Atlanta scored forty-seven.

The flight back to Green Bay was as silent as a tomb. I told Cherry that our performance the following week would tell me what kind of character we possessed, but I already knew what the answer was.

The Chicago Bears rumbled into Lambeau Field behind the leadership of Mike Ditka and the talent of Walter Payton. They were a fast-improving team and would have loved to nail us while we were down. Our players would have no part of it. We moved the ball up and down the field against Buddy Ryan's 46 defense and led, 28–14, in the fourth quarter. After nearly blowing the game, we finally defeated the Bears, 31–28, on yet another last-second field goal from Jan Stenerud.

Two weeks later, we traveled to Chicago for a rematch that would determine whether we made the playoffs for a second consecutive season. In sharp contrast to the mild conditions that prevailed in Green Bay, the weather in Chicago was almost intolerable for both teams. The temperature was in single digits and a cold wind from Lake Michigan ripped through the jerseys as the players prepared to warm up for the battle. The icy conditions favored the team that could run the ball. Advantage Bears and Walter Payton. The game meant more to us, however, since we were fighting for a playoff spot. Advantage Packers.

To the surprise of nobody, the game seesawed back and forth, before we took the lead, 21–20, with a few minutes left. If our defense could stop them, we were in the playoffs.

The Bears marched right downfield and kicked the winning field goal with ten seconds remaining.

Despite the emotionally draining defeat, I was proud of our accomplishments. We finished the season 8-8, yet we played just as well, considering the adversity we had to overcome as we did in 1982, when we came close to playing in the National Football Conference championship. We were no longer a losing ball club, and, more important, we were on the verge of long-term respectability. We had rekindled the emotions between the Packer fans and the team. We played exciting, hard-hitting football, and we did so with class. Unfortunately, the Packers had.a president who failed to recognize the importance of what we had achieved.

At 8:00 A.M. the day after our Bears game, Judge Parins walked into my office.

"I want to talk to you, Bart," he said.

I was on my way out to meet with our assistant coaches for a planning-and-review session.

"The coaches are waiting for me. Is it going to take long?" I asked.

"Not long at all," he replied. "You don't have to worry about your meeting, because as of this moment I am relieving you of your coaching position."

He didn't thank me for my efforts, didn't say a word about my twenty-six-year contribution to the Green Bay Packer organization. He didn't even express any regret about having to make the decision. He sounded as though he were delivering a cold, unemotional sentence in his circuit court.

*I am relieving you of your coaching position.* His words burned in my mind as he quickly turned around and walked out. I was furious about his lack of support. Finally, I felt shock, and I realized my relationship with the Packers was over. I closed the door to my office and cried.

# CHAPTER

## 17

*It must have been cold there in my shadow*
*To never have sunlight in your face*
*You have been content to let me shine*
*You always walked the step behind.*

*I was the one with all the glory*
*While you were the one with all the strength*
*Only a face without a name*
*I never once heard you complain.*

*Did you ever know that you're my hero*
*And everything I would like to be*
*I can fly higher than an eagle*
*Cause you're the wind beneath my wings.*

—JEFF SILBAR, LARRY HENLY
Warner House of Music, BMI
WB Gold Music, ASCAP

Those words appropriately convey my feelings about the greatest lady in the world and my best friend, Cherry. Read the lines again and you will begin to understand why my life has been so richly blessed during thirty-three years of marriage. During that time I have observed a very devoted mate and exceptional mother, a fastidious homemaker, great cook, and compassionate neighbor with great love for her community. Most of all, she has an enviable sense of humor.

After thirty-one years we have sold our home and are leaving Green Bay. We leave behind us volumes of memories—the births of our sons, their school years, the building of the home we have loved so much, the exciting Packer years, our dreams, and our disappointments. Above all else, we leave behind thirty-one years of friendships that have made living in such a small community so special.

A football career is tough on families. The incredibly long hours of preparation, the extreme highs and lows, the public demand of private time, are all part of a professional athlete's life-style. My family handled the pressures well partly because of Cherry's total commitment to our sons and me.

Our home was always the gathering place for our children's friends. I never knew how many boys would show up for breakfast—everyone was always welcome and made to feel part of our family. Sometimes there were children who simply did not have a loving home to go to after school. I remember one child when Bret was about ten or twelve who came home with him after school closed for Thanksgiving. When Cherry called to let his mother know where he was, she indicated she really did not care if her son came home, even though it was a traditional family holiday. Feeling sorry for the child, Cherry had him bathe, shampooed his hair, gave him a badly needed haircut, dressed him in one of Bret's suits, and brought him with our family to our annual Packer Thanksgiving dinner. Following dinner, on our way home in the car, he was so excited he did not stop talking. Sharing Thanksgiving dinner with all the players he idolized was beyond his wildest dreams.

Another young man, Kwomena Amoha came into our lives in 1978. We learned of his plight through a friend. He was a foreign student at University of Wisconsin–Green Bay who had lost his sponsorship and was about to be deported to his home in Ghana, where he had little hope of an education. He immediately became part of our family and has been able to finish his studies at the University of Chicago Medical School. Once, when he was home on vacation, Cherry was making arrangements to increase medical insurance benefits for our son Bart junior. An insurance agent, Rick Beverstein, was coming to our home to discuss options. Cherry and Kwomena, who is about five feet six and very dark-skinned, were waiting in the den. When Rick arrived, she escorted him into the den, looked at Kwomena and said,

"Mr. Beverstein, I would like you to meet our son Bart junior."
Kwomena hopped up, smiled, and shook his hand. Rick just
stood there for a moment and finally muttered, "Well, Bart,
you aren't exactly what I was expecting."

Cherry's sense of humor helped us weather many stress-
ful situations. She can find something amusing in almost
anything, which was usually, though not always, well received by our children. When Bret turned sixteen, he re-
quested a subscription to *Playboy* magazine. Every day, when
he came home from school, he checked the mailbox to see
if his first issue had arrived. The day it did, Cherry discovered a large photo in one of our tabloid newspapers of a
monkey from the San Diego Zoo that bore an amazing re-
semblance to the Ayatollah Khomenni. She took the *Playboy*
from the mailbox, glued the picture into the centerfold, put
the magazine back in its plain brown wrapper, and returned
it to the mailbox. When Bret came home, she watched him
check the mail. Trying to conceal his excitement, with his
magazine tucked safely between his books, he raced into the
house, went straight into his room, closed the door, and did
not speak to his mother for the rest of the week.

As an incentive for Bart junior to do well in school, I
promised him a dime for every perfect paper he brought
home. He must have laughed all the way to school the next
day, for I wasn't aware that my future *summa cum laude*
student had been bringing home perfect papers for two or
three years.

Returning home late one Sunday evening after winning
a big game against the Cardinals, I went into our bedroom,
turned down the bedspread, and found on my pillow a
shiny new dime—a special reward from a very proud son.

I was equally proud of him. When he was about ten, he
began playing golf with a close friend of ours, Lorraine Houston. She helped him develop an interest in the game, and
he eventually earned a golf scholarship to the University of
Alabama. While there, he continued to excel academically,
and graduated from Alabama's business school with highest
honors. Three years later, I watched him receive his diploma

from the University of Alabama School of Law. That day meant far more to me than any Super Bowl.

I also have the highest regard for Bart for the manner in which he has handled the attention and responsibility that comes with his name. He has always treated his family, friends, and associates with a tremendous amount of respect, recognizing that a person's greatest asset is his or her dignity.

Bart has been the beneficiary of good luck as well. While a junior at Alabama, he met a stunning redhead named Martha McShane. They immediately hit it off and eloped six months later. Cherry and I knew something about eloping ourselves and were delighted for them. Martha has been as special to Bart as Cherry has been to me. Cherry has said on numerous occasions that Bart junior could have searched the world over and not found a daughter-in-law who was more beautiful and loving and fit into our family so well. Whenever Cherry and I arrive in Franklin, Tennessee (a small town just south of Nashville), we are greeted by Shannon and Jennifer, their two precious daughters, who warm our hearts.

One of the fringe benefits of being a public figure is being recognized. I have had many interesting encounters with people over the years—some sad, some very amusing—I have always enjoyed meeting these folks and try to put them at ease if they seem nervous about approaching me. Adults often use their children as a buffer, even if they are reluctant. Cherry and I were passing through Chicago's O'Hare Airport once when we noticed a mother trying to persuade her young son to speak to me. She nudged him over and said to him, "Randy, please say hello to Bart Starr."

Randy looked up at me and said, in a voice heard by everyone within ten feet of us, "Fart who?"

Another reward of fame is receiving fascinating and entertaining mail. Requests for autographed photos are just a small segment of the mail athletes receive. People will ask for anything and everything. I have always acknowledged sincere requests to write letters of encouragement to someone who has suffered a disappointment or illness, and I always honor requests for personally autographed photos. Problems arise when fans forget to put a complete return address or the writing is so poor you can't read it. Cherry has spent hours trying to track down, by phone, a child whose address we could not decipher, so that child would not be let down. I always remembered my own son's hurt when he wrote a very famous baseball player, whom he much admired, and for weeks fruitlessly checked the mail for his photo, until he finally gave up.

I have saved many of my favorite letters. I loved the one that said, "Our teacher asked our class who was the greatest quarterback in the NFL. I said, 'Bart Starr,' and he just laughed." My very favorite was from a young lady who said, "Please send me two pictures for our school—one with your uniform on and one with it off. Love, Amy, age 9."

Some friends of ours attending a medical seminar in Japan decided for fun to send a note to me, but the only words they wrote on the outside of the envelope were "To the Greatest Quarterback in the World"—no name, city, or state. Miraculously, it was delivered to us in De Pere. When I arrived home late that evening, Cherry greeted me at the door and said, "Hi, honey. The most interesting thing happened today; you received a letter that was obviously intended for Johnny Unitas!"

Cherry's transition from player's wife to coach's wife was a natural one. She was accustomed to long hours alone, the pressures every Sunday, the scrunity of the public. She always believed in me, supported my choices and decisions, and was totally devoted to my chosen career.

One of the things I loved her most for was her willingness to give her time and concern to any of our players and their families whenever there was a need. She nursed them through illnesses, cooked for them, and even cleaned their homes in emergencies.

In 1980 tight end Bill Larson tore knee ligaments in the last game of the season and had to undergo surgery on Christmas Eve. Bill was prepared to spend the evening all alone, as his family was unable to get to Green Bay. Cherry

drove to every Christmas-tree lot in the city but could find
nothing open that late in the evening. She then drove to a
nursery, bought a three-foot Norwegian pine, and decorated it with tiny glass balls and icicles. Her next stop
was a local department store, where she purchased some
Christmas presents for Bill. Cherry parked her car a few
blocks from the hospital and trudged through the snow,
battling temperatures below zero. Once inside, she discovered that she was at the wrong hospital. Cherry was
undeterred. She gathered the presents and the tree and
walked a few more blocks to the other hospital. When Bill
awoke from his operation, the tree and the presents and
Cherry were there to greet him.

Bill's knee never regained the strength required to play
football again, but he treasured Cherry's thoughtfulness. The
following summer, we received a huge box at our home. We
opened it and saw the best-looking corn on the cob you can
imagine. Bill's parents, who were Iowa farmers, let us know
that they, too, appreciated Cherry's gesture.

Once she persuaded me to make an exception to a team
rule and take a player's wife to Tampa on the team plane.
Cherry knew she was very ill and wanted to do something
special for her. I told the players why I had decided to take
her along. As she slowly entered the plane, every player
stood and cheered. It was one of the most touching gestures
I have ever witnessed, and her husband was overcome with
emotion. Cherry spent almost every minute with her, attending to all her needs and arranging for a seat next to her
in the visiting owner's box. Though the trip was physically
exhausting to her, the young wife had a wonderful time and
thanked me profusely on the return trip. Burnedette Thompson, wife of our wide receiver Aundra Thompson, died a
few months later from multiple sclerosis.

It wouldn't be appropriate for a discussion of Cherry to
end on a sad note, however. She is too upbeat, warm, and
just plain crazy. We were in Phoenix recently to see John
Colbrunn, one of the partners in our group that is seeking
an NFL expansion franchise in that city. I left early one

morning for a speaking engagement in Florida; Cherry was
flying to Denver that afternoon. John, who lives in Colorado
Springs, was scheduled to depart at about the same time.

John accompanied her on the airline bus to the Phoenix
airport, walked her to her gate, and gave her a hug and kiss
good-bye. Cherry sat down beside a man who had been on
the same bus. Before long, he struck up a conversation.

"Do you live in Denver?" he asked.

"No," she replied, "I live in Green Bay, Wisconsin."

"Green Bay? Have you ever seen Bart Starr?" he inquired.

Cherry had the man right where she wanted. "Oh, I've
seen him from time to time."

The man, now consumed with curiosity, asked, "Have
you ever had a chance to TALK to him?"

Cherry nodded and responded, "Yes, on many occasions." She then leaned over and whispered, "As a matter
of fact, I slept with him last night." The poor man didn't
know what to say until Cherry finally burst out laughing and
introduced herself.

No chapter concerning our family would be complete
without a discussion of the heartaches, frustration, and eventual growth that we have experienced as a result of our younger
son's use of drugs.

From the time he was a child, Bret had difficulty dealing with being Bart Starr's son in a small community. While
Bart junior grew up during the Packers' exciting glory
years, Bret was, at a very sensitive age, living with his family
through seasons of disappointments and frequent criticism
of his father by the news media. It was not a happy time for
any of us, especially Bret, who had to face his peers every
Monday

Bret has a brilliant mind, but unlike Bart junior, who
was very self-motivated and successful in almost everything
he did, Bret lacked interest in school and sports. A gifted
guitarist, he turned his interest to rock music, motorcycles,
and reptiles. These activities led him to some pretty unde-
sirable characters. Specifically, he began associating with
potheads.

Looking back, there were definite signs. Bret was experimenting with drugs, but Cherry and I were in a denial stage, unable to believe our young son could possibly be involved in anything so ugly. Unbeknownst to us, by the time Bret graduated from high school, he was well on his way to cocaine addiction.

He enrolled in a preveterinary program at the University of Wisconsin and quickly deteriorated. The pressure of Wisconsin's rigorous academic requirements, combined with the widespread accessibility of drugs, compounded his already perilous chemical dependency.

Cherry's concern for Bret was growing stronger but, knowing how hard I was working to rebuild the Packers, she tried to deal with Bret alone. But she was unable to conceal her fears any longer when I came home one night to find her sobbing. She told me Bret wasn't doing well in school and did not seem coherent when she spoke to him by phone. We dropped everything and drove to Madison the next day. We went directly to his dorm and knocked on the door. He asked, "Who's there?" When we answered, he refused to let us in. When he finally relented, we got the shock of our lives. The son we adored so much was standing before us looking like a frightened, hunted animal. Cherry and I had never experienced such pain as we felt at that moment.

We brought Bret home, and arranged for him to be admitted to Hazelden drug rehabilitation center in Minneapolis. Two days after his admission we received a call from a nurse there, saying we should come and get Bret because he was not adapting well to group therapy. When we arrived the next day, he was so pathetic. He hugged us and cried and promised to help himself if he could come home. We enlisted the help of a local drug therapist and Bret did seem to make excellent progress. We thought our nightmare was over.

Confident he had his problem under control, we agreed to help finance Bret and a friend in an exotic-animal import business in Tampa, Florida. I have no idea now why we thought he could succeed in business with no training, but

we loved him so much we were willing to do anything to
help him pursue a field he really enjoyed. It did not take
long for Bret to find a new source of drugs, for his new partner
himself had a heavy drug addiction. Our nightmare began
again.

Broken promises, deceptions, failure to return phone calls,
unacknowledged birthdays and holidays were all part of the
scenario—things were worse than ever. The strain of dealing
with Bret's problems were taking a terrible toll on Cherry
and me. There were moments when we felt absolutely help-
less but we loved our son and could not give up an attempt
to help him. Our search for help led us to Dr. Ed Klein, who
had enjoyed much success working with drug addiction in
the Tampa area. He agreed to see Bret. Though Bret really
liked Dr. Klein, things did not go well—there were missed
appointments, faked urinalysis results, deceptions, and ma-
nipulations. Cherry and I felt desperate. His life and ours
seemed out of control. We both were depressed, angry, and
frustrated. We did not know where to turn next. When we
least expected it a call came from Bret. He had seen Dr. Klein
on television talking about drug addiction and the pain it
caused so many people. Something hit. He was crying so
hard he could hardly speak. He said, "Mom, I want to get
this shit out of my life." He did; he quit cold turkey that
day. He sought a new outlet by turning to a demanding body-
building program and put his trust in God to get him through
each day, always remembering to thank Him each night for
the strength he was receiving. He called home almost daily
to receive the support he knew he could also depend on
from us.

In 1986, for the first time in three years he agreed to join
our family for Christmas. Since we were gathering at Bart
junior and Martha's home in Franklin, we sent Bret an airline
ticket to join us there. We were not convinced Bret would
actually show up. We were almost conditioned to the past
disappointments. Though Bret was getting his life in order,
his paranoia about travel and public places was still a mit-
igating factor. On his way to the Tampa airport Bret stopped

at a phone booth to call Cherry and tell her he had been involved in an accident and was going to miss his flight. He put in the quarter, dialed the number, and let it ring. Before Cherry answered, he hung up. Getting on that airplane was one of the most difficult things he ever did.

Bart junior greeted his younger brother at the Nashville airport with a loving hug. Bret was outgoing, personable, funny. He told his brother everything about his drug habit; Bart told him how proud he was of his determination to beat it. Bret was working at becoming a power lifter, but his inner strength was even more impressive. None of his problems could stand up to this accomplishment.

Bret walked in Bart and Martha's house with a huge smile on his face. Cherry and I could hardly stop hugging him. His nieces were equally delighted to see him, and he'd brought them two rare spotted tortoises.

As our family gathered in the den to open a few presents, Bret handed Cherry a card. She opened it, read the first line, and stopped. "I have something I would like to read to everyone," she said. Her eyes were already moist and her voice a little shaky, but she managed to read Bret's personal message:

Dear Mom and Dad,
    The patience and understanding you showed during my problems means more than you will ever know. Without your love and caring, I could never have gotten over it. You stood by me when most parents would have finally turned their backs. I love you so much for that and can finally understand that you are truly my two best friends.

Love,<br>Bret

It was the best Christmas present we've ever received.

My last story is a happy one. On May 8, 1979, Cherry and I celebrated our twenty-fifth wedding anniversary.

The previous five or six years had been very hard on my family. The two years I spent out of football between my retirement as a player and accepting the coaching position were not happy times for me. I never realized how much I would miss being actively involved in the game I loved so much. I committed myself to too many engagements, worked weekends for CBS, promoted my business interests, and answered every charitable cause I could handle. It was as though I could not find enough to fill the void left when I retired from football. My family suffered—I simply was never home. It was Cherry's total responsibility to run our home and attend to all of Bart's and Bret's needs, all week and weekends, too. When the Packer coaching opportunity came along, my responsibilities grew larger—long hours, weekend travel, and enormous stress on everyone.

I could not have asked for a more supportive wife during these times. She did everything she could to provide a happy, stable atmosphere for all of us. I could see an opportunity coming up to show her how much I appreciated her.

The 1979 NFL league meetings were being held in Hawaii that year. Without Cherry's knowledge, I arranged for us to renew our wedding vows at the Fern Grotto on the island of Kauai. A gorgeous spot, people come from all over the world to be married there. Our two closest friends from Green Bay, Gary and Emily Knafelc, aware of my plan, joined us for a week in Hawaii. The only thing Cherry knew was that we were going somewhere special one evening and she should take along a long dress.

The scene was like something from a movie. A glorious day, Hawaiian chanters entertained us while we sailed up the river to the Grotto. It was an incredible sight. Tiny candles among the most beautiful flowers and vegetation made the perfect romantic setting. We were greeted by a full-blooded Hawaiian minister, who performed a lovely ceremony while the chanters sang the "Hawaiian Wedding Song." Gary and Emily were beside us sharing that special moment in our lives.

It could not have been a more perfect way for me to

express my appreciation to Cherry for her love, support, and unfailing loyalty for so many years.

After dinner that evening, Cherry and I returned to our beautifully decorated honeymoon suite. Feeling extremely romantic, I was doing everything possible to set the mood for the night—inviting Cherry to the couch, turning off the lights, and whispering to her how very much I loved her. Things were going very well when the phone rang. I leaped to my feet and there was a tremendous crash. Cherry quickly turned on the light, and there I was sprawled naked on the floor, having tripped over a full-size wooden leopard I had forgotten was in the room. Cherry became hysterical with laughter. Because of her great sense of humor, it really was the perfect ending to a very special day.